Wild Places
Quiet Places

Published by Dr Syd Shea, Executive Director, Department of Conservation and Land Management,
Technology Park, Western precinct, Dick Perry Avenue, Kensington, Western Australia, 6151.

Managing Editor: Ron Kawalilak

Editors: Carolyn Thomson-Dans, Mitzi Vance

Designer: Sue Marais

Cartography: Mark Lamming and Holly Smith from the GIS section of CALM's Information Management Branch

Contributors: Rod Annear, Roger Banks, Jennifer Brice, Andrew Cribb, Peter Dans, Steve Dutton, Peter Henderson, Ian Herford, Colleen Henry-Hall, Annie Keating, Daryl Moncrieff, Terry Passmore, Tammie Reid, Phil Spencer, Neil Taylor, Klaus Tiedeman, Trevor Walley, John Watson, Glenn Wilmott, Cliff Winfield

ISBN 0 7309 6871 5

DEPARTMENT OF CONSERVATION AND LAND MANAGEMENT

WILD PLACES, QUIET PLACES

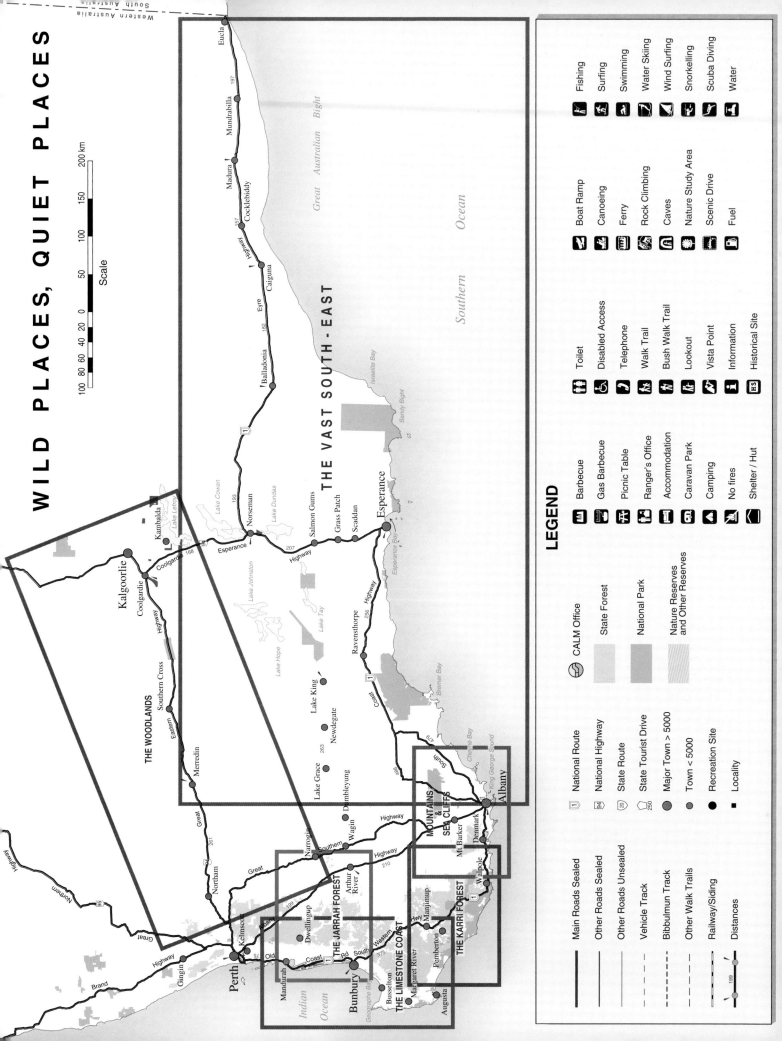

LEGEND

ⓢ	CALM Office
	State Forest
	National Park
	Nature Reserves and Other Reserves

▬	Main Roads Sealed		🅐	National Route
▬	Other Roads Sealed		🅐	National Highway
▬	Other Roads Unsealed		🅐	State Route
▬	Vehicle Track		⬡	State Tourist Drive
▬	Bibbulmun Track		⬤	Major Town > 5000
▬	Other Walk Trails		⬤	Town < 5000
▬	Railway/Siding		⬤	Recreation Site
▬	Distances		■	Locality

🄱	Barbecue		🚻	Toilet
	Gas Barbecue		🚻	Disabled Access
🄿	Picnic Table		☎	Telephone
	Ranger's Office		🚶	Walk Trail
	Accommodation		🚶	Bush Walk Trail
🄒	Caravan Park			Lookout
	Camping			Vista Point
	No fires		ℹ	Information
	Shelter / Hut		HS	Historical Site

	Boat Ramp			Fishing
	Canoeing			Surfing
	Ferry			Swimming
	Rock Climbing			Water Skiing
	Caves			Wind Surfing
	Nature Study Area			Snorkelling
	Scenic Drive			Scuba Diving
	Fuel			Water

Contents

East Mount Barren, Fitzgerald River National Park. Photo – Bill Belson/Lochman Transparencies

Wild Places
Quiet Places

The southern half of Western Australia is rich in beauty and contrast, and is a perfect escape for people seeking adventure in the great outdoors. The national parks, State forests and reserves of the South-West, South Coast, Wheatbelt and Goldfields offer an almost limitless range of options for weekend escapes, day trips or touring holidays.

In the South-West corner, between Perth and Walpole, tall forests, winding rivers, waterfalls and wild beautiful beaches create a stunning environment. The famous Tree Top Walk at the Valley of the Giants in Walpole-Nornalup National Park rises almost 40 metres above the forest floor. At ground level, a walktrail travels right through some of the natural hollows in the old tingle trees.

Near Albany, on the South Coast, dramatic coastal cliffs overlook the cold Southern Ocean, while inland the towering peaks of the Stirling Range, and the forested outcrops of the Porongurup Range rise out of the flat land of the Great Southern agricultural district.

From Bremer Bay to Eucla in the far south, windswept heaths cover rolling coastal plains that stretch to the horizon. Forty million years ago the Eocene sea inundated these plains, turning the ancient hills into islands. They are inhabited by native plants and animals, many confined to tiny pockets of suitable habitat. Some of these plants and animals are endangered, and many are found nowhere else on the planet.

Take a driving tour and discover the vast South Coast, or take a week and go camping in the karri forest. Enjoy the smell of wood smoke from the campfire, and the joy of a clear morning in the bush. Catch a fish, discover a place you've never seen before, or soak in the wonder of the spectacular sunsets.

Sunset at Victoria Rock Nature Reserve. Photo – Jay Sarson/Lochman Transparencies

Enjoying natural areas

CAMPING

In an effort to protect our environment, visitors may only camp at designated camping sites – usually marked with a sign in national parks, State forests or bush areas. Please leave no rubbish or other traces of your visit. Camping fees are charged in some areas and the funds raised help to pay for the facilities and services provided.

BUSHWALKING

There are walktrails in many parks and forests. These vary from short strolls to long distance hikes through rugged country (see The Bibbulmun Track on page 14). Check information panels or ask staff from the Department of Conservation and Land Management (CALM) for details.

Choose walks to suit your level of fitness, and for comfort and safety wear sturdy shoes or boots and a hat, and apply sunscreen. For longer walks, carry a good map, a compass and plenty of water. Tell someone where you are going and when you intend to be back.

CALM produces a great range of publications on bushwalking in the South-West. Visit CALM's secure on-line bookshop (see page 19) or call (08) 9334 0333 for details of stockists.

CARAVANS

Commercial caravan parks operate in towns near most parks and some forests. Only a few national parks have powered van sites and hot water. Check with the WA Tourist Centre or local tourist information centres for details of commercial caravan parks.

ENTRY FEES

Day visitor fees apply at many national parks, and may be collected at entry points by park rangers or left in collection boxes on an honesty basis. Fees help to manage the areas from where they are collected and are used to provide better facilities for park visitors.

A range of passes available from CALM provide a cost effective means of enjoying national parks. The Holiday Pass allows entry to all parks for up to four weeks, and represents excellent value for people on holidays. The Annual Pass is ideal for people who may regularly visit one park. The All Parks Annual Local Park Pass entitles holders entry to all national parks for 12 months, while the Gold Star Pass offers entry to all national parks for 12 months plus an annual subscription to CALM's award-winning *LANDSCOPE* magazine. Park passes are available from most tourist information centres, CALM's *WA Naturally* outdoors information centre, CALM offices and CALM's secure on-line bookshop.

A number of exceptions and fee concessions apply. Cyclists and walkers do not have to pay entry fees. Licensed recreational fishers who visit a national park in order to fish are also exempt. Discounts apply to senior card and aged pension card holders. Further enquiries about concessions can be directed to the nearest CALM office (see page 148).

FOUR-WHEEL-DRIVING

Four-wheel-driving is particularly popular in the State's South Coast region, from Augusta to east of Esperance, as well as in the Goldfields.

A few simple precautions will help to protect the environment and ensure tracks don't get chopped up, while making the journey easier on both driver and vehicle.

- All four-wheel-drive vehicles should carry a tyre pressure gauge and pump or air-compressor, so the tyres can be deflated or inflated as the need arises.
- For improved traction on some track surfaces, and especially when travelling on sand, it is wise to lower tyre pressures to increase tyre footprint. Under certain conditions, it may be necessary to deflate tyres to extra low pressures in the sand, to enable the vehicle to traverse areas without becoming bogged. The amount that you should deflate the tyres will vary with the size and type of tyres and the weight of your vehicle. For example, tyres with 'rigid sidewalls' may need to be deflated more than tyres with 'soft sidewalls' to achieve the required footprint. Drive at slow speed while the tyres are deflated, as potential exists for tyres to separate from rims under stress. Deflated tyres should be inflated to appropriate pressure as soon as possible after clearing the obstacle.
- Engage four-wheel-drive before you reach the sand.
- Select the right gear to avoid having trouble changing gears in loose sand. You may have to experiment a little, but for most vehicles low range third will keep you moving at a comfortable pace. It also has enough power not to stall when the going gets heavier.
- Use existing tracks. Don't create new ones or drive on scrub. You will destroy the plants, and could also stake your tyres.
- Where beaches are open to vehicles, access is restricted to the area between the low water mark and the start of the first vegetated dunes. Do not 'cut up' on the dunes.
- Remember that all drivers and vehicles (including motorbikes and dune buggies) must be registered for the road and licensed. National parks are not off-road vehicle areas.
- Stay safe and don't speed along narrow one-lane tracks.
- Take heed of management signs erected for both your benefit and to protect the environment.

NATIVE PLANTS AND ANIMALS

In order to protect the environment, please do not disturb any native animals, and do not pick wildflowers. Rocks, vegetation or old logs should not be removed, as these often house small creatures that depend on such habitats for existence.

Top right: Young numbats.
Right: Western grey kangaroo. Photos – Jiri Lochman

WATER

Most creeks and rivers in Western Australia are dry during the summer. When you are touring, take your own drinking water. If you do have to use water from the few permanent water points, it should be boiled before use, or purified using a commercially available purification product.

CARING FOR THE BUSH

Special care is needed to protect our natural environment for future generations to enjoy. Many areas are fragile, and tramping your own path through the bush can result in long-term damage. By remembering a few basic rules, you can do your bit to protect the environment.

- Stay on paths and help to prevent erosion.
- Take special care in sensitive areas, such as sand dunes, and areas with steep slopes or sparse vegetation.
- Wash at least 100 metres away from streams, rivers and lakes. Detergents and toothpaste harm aquatic life.
- Use sand instead of detergent to wash your dishes and keep rubbish or food scraps out of streams, rivers and lakes.

FISHING

You are welcome to fish in national parks and forests, but you may need a licence. Marron fishing is a seasonal activity by permit only. Trout and redfin perch are present in some inland waters. For the latest information on fishing regulations and licenses, contact Fisheries Western Australia on (08) 9482 7333.

FIRE

Bushfires are a real danger, particularly during the dry summer months.

- Always use fireplaces where they are provided. Better still, bring your own portable stove.
- Open fires are not permitted in most national parks. However, where fireplaces are provided, you must collect wood (fallen timber only) from outside the park or bring it from home.
- Clear all leaf litter, dead branches and anything else that may burn from an area at least three metres around and above fires and portable stoves.
- Never leave a fire unattended.
- Make sure the fire is completely out before leaving. If the ground underneath is still warm, the fire is not out. Use soil and water to extinguish the embers, and bury the ashes.

On some days, especially in summer, the fire forecast may be 'very high' or 'extreme'. A total fire ban exists on these days and some paths or even whole reserves may be closed as a safety precaution. Local radio stations broadcast fire risk warnings, but please check with local government authorities, tourist information centres, or the nearest CALM office for advice on the fire situation.

Fishing for trout in Lefroy Brook, near Pemberton. Photo – Jiri Lochman

PETS

Pets are not permitted in national parks, nature reserves and water catchments. Many other parks and reserves managed by local government authorities do not allow pets. If you are not sure whether dogs and/or other pets are permitted at the place you intend to visit, please leave them at home. See the section about *Western Shield* on page 12 for further information about poison baits laid in parks and forests to protect local wildlife. These baits are lethal to domestic pets. Watch out for warning signs that indicate an area has been baited.

VEHICLES

Normal road rules apply in all recreation and conservation areas. To protect wildlife habitat and the environment from erosion and dieback disease, please keep to formed roads and designated tracks at all times. Be sure to lock your vehicle if it is left unattended. Remember that all drivers and vehicles (including motorbikes and dune buggies) must be registered for the road.

RUBBISH

Place all litter in bins provided. If there are no bins, take your litter home with you. When camping or walking in the bush, bury organic waste at least 15 centimetres deep and at least 100 metres from any waterway, picnic area or campsite. Never throw rubbish overboard while boating – plastics and other rubbish can kill marine animals.

DIEBACK

Some areas of forest and woodland have been infected by a soil-borne fungus (*Phytophthora cinnamomi*) that attacks the root systems of trees, shrubs and wildflowers. The disease is known to attack at least 900 plant species and many, such as banksias and dryandras, die very quickly. The fungus travels over and through the soil in water, attaching spores to roots. The rot sets in immediately.

The fungus is carried in soil or mud that sticks to boots and shoes, and the wheels, mudguards and underbodies of vehicles. When the soil or mud drops off, the fungus immediately contaminates the new area and multiplies. There is, as yet, no known broad-scale cure.

Some areas in national parks and State forests are closed to vehicles to prevent dieback being carried into or spread through them. These areas are largely uninfected. You may enter on foot but you must not take vehicles, motorbikes, horses or any form of wheeled transport into these areas. When walking through infected areas, help stop the rot by not straying from the track. Observe the signs and give our plants a chance.

We hope you enjoy WA's national parks and forests. Check out CALM's award-winning range of publications to help you get the most out of your visit. Or you can keep up-to-date by subscribing to CALM's *LANDSCOPE* magazine. For information call (08) 9334 0333, call into CALM's *WA Naturally* information centre (see page 13), or visit the Department's website (see page 19).

*Showy banksia (*B. speciosa*) destroyed by dieback disease. Photo – Jiri Lochman*

Staying alive in the bush

PLANNING

The South-West is one of the most populated areas outside the Perth metropolitan area, yet some places are still wild and remote.

Planning is essential to any trip. Always tell someone where you're going and when you plan to be back. And don't forget to contact them when you've returned safely. By contacting the local Department of Conservation and Land Management (CALM) offices you also get up-to-date information on local conditions, an important supplement to maps.

Take your vehicle in for a complete check before you leave. Plan your route carefully. Know where you're going to stay, how long it will take you to get there and what gear you'll need once you've arrived. Carry water in case you get lost or your vehicle breaks down.

Don't venture anywhere without the right maps. RAC road maps are sufficient if you plan to stay on recognised roads. But if you get off the beaten track, you'll discover the bush is criss-crossed with tracks and can confuse you. Detailed maps (1:50 000), for most of the South-West forest, showing these tracks are available from CALM.

If you do get lost, stay on the best defined track. If you systematically follow well-travelled tracks, you will eventually end up at some habitation. If you are planning to go into remote or sparsely inhabited areas, it's a good idea to read up on survival skills before your trip or do a bush survival course.

COPING WITH EMERGENCIES

If your car breaks down, do not leave it to search for help. If you have informed someone of your whereabouts, help will be along soon, and it's always easier to spot a car than a person.

Your first survival consideration is water. Permanent water sources are marked on CALM maps, but much of this water is not suitable for drinking. Boil it for at least 10 minutes, or sterilise it with water purification tablets. Secure a plastic bag around a bunch of leaves on a tree to collect the water that is transpired by the tree. Try digging in dry creek beds, but not in the heat of the day. Water can be extracted from mud or sand by soaking a rag and wringing it out into a container.

Other considerations, especially in the cool South-West, are shelter and warmth. One of the best things you can take on a camping or bushwalking trip is a space blanket. Light and portable, it can be warm or cool, depending on which side faces outward. Your car is an excellent form of shelter.

Warmth is important. It is easiest to light a fire with matches or a lighter, but, lacking these, turn to your car again. You can start a fire with the cigarette lighter and a petrol-soaked rag. Another way is to remove the battery, attach fine wire to both terminals and touch the ends of the wire together to produce a spark, but be careful, as car batteries produce a highly volatile gas.

Fire can be essential to survival, but it can also be life threatening. Under most circumstances, use gas or fuel stoves. Fire should only be used when strictly necessary and it should be used with caution.

BUSHFIRE SURVIVAL

Bushfires are a threat. Days or weeks of hot, dry conditions and strong winds increase the danger. By the end of summer, the forest can be a tinderbox.

The main cause of death in a bushfire is heat radiation, rather than direct contact with flames or lack of oxygen. As bushfires move rapidly, the peak only lasts for a few minutes. Plan to survive those crucial few minutes:

- Don't panic. It drains physical and nervous energy and clouds your judgement.
- Your car is a safe refuge. Do not drive blindly through smoke. Switch on your headlights and park on a bare area beside the road on the opposite side to a fire.
- Wind up the windows and shelter from the heat beneath the dashboard with a rug, floor mat, anything, covering your body.
- The petrol tank will not explode, and even in the worst situations it will be some moments before the vehicle catches alight. If the car does not catch fire, get out after the peak fire has passed, but keep your skin covered as much as possible.

Living Windows: a natural experience

The South-West offers natural experiences found nowhere else in the world. Reclusive and rare animals, majestic birds of prey, wild dolphins, wetland habitats, towering forests, incredible caves and unique wildflowers are just a few of the diverse natural attractions you can enjoy.

Living Windows sites – windows into the world of nature – are located throughout the South-West. Living Windows provide fascinating insights into the natural and cultural environment. They allow you to step into each habitat and see the birds, animals and marine life in their own environment. Many Living Windows have audiovisual presentations, interpretive information and interactive displays. The following Living Windows take you from marine and coastal environments to wetlands, limestone caves and through jarrah, karri and tingle forests:

Valley of the Giants Tree Top Walk – Gain a bird's eye view of towering tingle forest from a spectacular lightweight bridge through the forest canopy. See page 98.

Caveworks – Hidden caves reveal vast chambers, fossil remains and stunning crystalline formations. Above ground, an interpretive centre provides a range of interactive multimedia educational attractions. See page 69.

Dolphin Discovery Centre – Wild dolphins visit a Bunbury bay almost every day to interact with people. An interpretive centre details the habits of these highly intelligent mammals. See page 58.

Ngilgi Cave – Take a journey above and beneath the earth, where Aboriginal legend and a beautiful cave have a fascinating interplay. Below ground, there are cave adventure tours and torchlight tours. Above ground there are Aboriginal culture tours and walktrails. See page 65.

Eagles Heritage Raptor Wildlife Centre – The Centre boasts 80 Australian birds of prey. Set among 12 hectares of bush, visitors can watch free-flight displays of captive-bred birds and also witness snake handling.

Karri Forest Discovery Centre – Walk through a discovery garden which depicts the understorey of a karri forest, which changes with the seasons. Also explore the karri forest through a 122 hectare forest park and walktrails. See page 84.

Forest Heritage Centre – This unique leaf-shaped building is surrounded by jarrah forest walks, including a walk through the canopy of the trees. Explore traditional Aboriginal use of the forest and a timbergetter's hut from the early 1900s. See page 38.

Lighthouse and Discovery Centre – The historic Cape Naturaliste lighthouse, on a rugged promontory, is surrounded by diverse plants and animals.

Perup Wilderness Lodge – Special hideaways and walks provide the opportunity to view rare marsupials and more common species at night. See page 83.

RGC Wetlands Centre – Near the South-West town of Capel, 14 wetlands developed from rehabilitated mine pits are now a haven for 50 species of waterbirds and 60 species of bush birds.

Eco Cultural Discovery Centre – The centre depicts the unique heritage of Greenbushes, a town with a history of tin mining, timber milling and farming.

Forest Trails – Walk among giant karri and jarrah trees which are centuries old, and experience the amazing understorey of the forests and local ecology.

Wellington Discovery Forest – Take a fascinating journey into the diverse ecosystem of a jarrah forest. Learn about the forest and how it is managed. See page 44.

Tuart Forest Visitor Centre – Explore the natural appeal of the coastal tuart woodland, with its friendly animals and subtle flora.

The Tree Top Walk in the Valley of the Giants, Walpole-Nornalup National Park. Photo – Michael James

Western Shield

The Department of Conservation and Land Management is currently undertaking the world's biggest campaign against feral predators, known as *Western Shield*. This wildlife recovery program aims to bring native animals back from the brink of extinction by controlling introduced predators. Introduced foxes and cats have already contributed to the extinction of 10 native mammal species, with dozens more species fighting for survival.

KEEPING PETS SAFE

Under *Western Shield*, CALM aims to reduce feral cat and fox populations through baiting programs using 1080 poisoning. This is the manufactured version of a poison that occurs naturally in the native plant genus *Gastrolobium*, commonly called 'poison peas'. This poison is lethal to introduced predators but does not harm native animals, which have evolved with the poison plants.

However, dogs and cats are very susceptible to 1080 poisoning, for which there is no antidote. Warning signs are placed prominently around baited areas, so visitors know baits are around, and advertisements are placed in all local newspapers. Domestic dogs and cats should not be allowed to roam in areas that have been baited.

BAITING SUCCESS

Since the project began, *Western Shield* has had astounding success. Comprehensive aerial baiting on more than 3.5 million hectares of CALM-managed lands has significantly reduced fox numbers. Native animal populations have begun to show signs of recovery, with monitoring and trapping of baited areas showing increases in native animal numbers and types.

To further restore native wildlife, CALM has begun recovery plans for a number of endangered species, such as the chuditch, numbat, bilby and western-barred bandicoot. These plans include captive breeding to increase species' populations and the release of animals into areas within their former home ranges. All such reintroductions are comprehensively monitored by CALM staff using techniques such as radio-collaring and tracking.

For instance, numbats have been released at Mt Dale in the Perth hills, chuditch have been returned to Cape Arid National Park, quendas (also known as southern brown bandicoots) were restored to Dongolocking Nature Reserve in the Wheatbelt, woylies and malleefowl were reintroduced to Shark Bay's Peron Peninsula as part of *Project Eden* (a sub-program of *Western Shield*), and noisy scrub-birds have been released in the Darling Range, where they were first discovered 150 years ago.

Western Shield has been so successful that three mammal species have experienced significant increases in population numbers. As a result, the woylie, tammar wallaby and quenda had been removed from the State's Threatened Species List by 1998.

A significant part of the project's success has been the support of local residents, farmers and private landowners. Support has also been received from the private sector with sponsorship from Cable Sands Pty Ltd, Alcoa of Australia and Westralian Sands Ltd.

Woylie. Photo – Jiri Lochman

Chuditch. Photo – Jiri Lochman

WA Naturally

The Department of Conservation and Land Management's *WA Naturally* outdoors and nature information centre allows visitors of all ages to learn more about Western Australia and its unique wildlife.

WA Naturally provides a point of contact and a source of information on conservation and land management in Western Australia. It stocks a complete selection of CALM's spectacular and award-winning nature publications, including the popular **Bush Books** (see page 18), guide books, recreation books, *LANDSCOPE* magazine, brochures and maps.

WA Naturally provides free access, via computer terminals, to the *NatureBase* web site and CALM's CD-ROM, *Wild about Western Australia,* which helps visitors to escape to some of the State's best nature spots via one of the terminals.

WA Naturally is housed within historic buildings in the University of Notre Dame complex at 47 Henry Street, Fremantle, phone (08) 9430 8600. Its unique design incorporates a life-sized boab tree, which appears to grow, through walls and barriers, into the foyer of the building. *WA Naturally* is open every day except Tuesday.

The Bibbulmun Track

The Bibbulmun Track, a 950 kilometre walktrail from Perth to Albany, is one of the great long-distance walktrails of the world.

Begun in the 1970s by the former Forests Department, the track was first upgraded in 1988. A major realignment by CALM began in 1993, to enhance the experience and enjoyment of walkers, and was completed in 1998. The new route takes walkers through some of the most scenic parts of the South-West, including the Monadnocks, Lane Poole and Noggerup conservation parks, Donnelly River Valley, Shannon National Park, D'Entrecasteaux National Park and Walpole-Nornalup National Park.

The Bibbulmun Track is named after a distinct Aboriginal language group which inhabited some of the areas on the South Coast through which the track passes. The Bibbulmun people often travelled for great distances to attend tribal meetings or to hunt, but the track doesn't follow any traditional route. The Bibbulmun language influenced place names across the South-West.

The Bibbulmun Track is suitable for use by a wide range of community and school groups, recreational walkers (day or weekend walks), experienced walkers (including long distance journeys) and visitors who may only have an hour or two to experience the natural beauty of the South-West of Western Australia.

There are 48 new campsites on the upgraded track, spaced between 10 and 20 kilometres apart, or roughly a day's walk. These campsites have timber sleeping shelters, tent sites, rainwater tanks, bush toilets and picnic tables. Some also have fireplaces. The shelters are available on a first-come, first-served basis.

The Track is designated only as a walktrail, and mountain bikes are not permitted. Some campsites are 'no fire' sites because of special risks which fire might impose in some particularly sensitive locations. From the Shannon River through to Albany, all campsites are 'fuel stove only', with no barbecues. This whole coastal area has high conservation values, minimum amounts of fuel or a combination of these.

Detailed maps and guide books for the Track are available at most good bookshops, backpacking equipment shops, CALM offices and CALM's *WA Naturally* outdoor information centre.

For details of stockists call (08) 9334 0333.

Right: Bibbulmun Track, Waaleeh camp site. Photo – Chris Garnett

Aboriginal tourism: sharing the Dreaming

Aboriginal people of the South-West are known as Nyoongar, but the group is made up of people who speak several different dialects of the Nyoongar language. People from the Kalgoorlie area are from the Wongi group, which is also made up people who speak different dialects of the Western Desert language.

TRADITIONAL LIFESTYLE

Aboriginal people of the South-West had a very ordered way of life. Their patterns of hunting and gathering were guided by six weather-based seasons. Nyoongar people did not measure time in weeks, months or years. Their 'year' was divided into seasons, according to the cycle of weather and the availability of food.

Each Nyoongar group had their 'kaleep', or favourite camping spot, which held special significance for them. Beyond this there was a more extensive area where they hunted and foraged. They travelled in small family groups, and only met in large clan groups a few times each year for ceremonies and to trade. Family units travelled within their defined territories, setting up camps for as long as the seasonal foods lasted. When special harvest foods were abundant, other Nyoongar groups were invited to share them.

Fish and other aquatic foods were seasonal mainstays of the traditional diet of people living in the coastal districts. The hunter-gatherers speared and trapped great quantities of fish in rivers and estuaries and collected a wide variety of foods from wetlands, including ducks and other waterfowl, tortoises, frogs and the edible roots of rushes. They set up fish traps using branches, creepers and stones across shallow waters. Fish would enter the trap at high tide, and Aboriginal people would spear or catch the fish using their hands. The quantities of fish caught from the largest of these weirs sometimes enabled hundreds of people to congregate for days on end to trade, to conduct marriages and initiations, and to carry out other cultural activities.

As there was no means of storing or preserving food for long periods, food gathering was a daily task. The women provided the vegetable content of the diet by gathering roots, seeds, fruits, tubers and bulbs. Like the men, they usually worked in groups. Favourites included the fruits of the quandong (*Santalum acuminatum*) and the yam-like tuber called warrn (*Dioscorea hastifolia*). They would also kill small game or lizards, including yuundaq (goanna) and yearn (bobtail lizard).

Cloaks made from kangaroo skins stitched together were worn by both sexes. The Nyoongar people built temporary, but weatherproof, huts (semi-circular domes of paperbark or grass tree thatch across a framework of tied branches).

All Aboriginal people across the South-West belonged to one of two skin classes. Members of the same skin class could not marry, and punishment was harsh for those who did not obey this law. There were very strict rules in marriage, and girls were betrothed before they were born. Their first husbands were often older men with several wives. When a man died, his younger wives usually lived with their father's tribe during the period of mourning, but it was not uncommon for them to live with the relatives of the husband. After the period of mourning, the younger wives often remarried.

THE DREAMING

Australian Aboriginal people have the longest continuous cultural history in the world. One of the features of their culture is their intense spiritual link to the land. Aboriginal people are bound to the land by ties which extend back to a time known as the Dreaming.

For Aboriginal people, the Dreaming explains the creation of nature and how all the parts are linked. They believe that people, other animals, plants, the sun, wind and rain are all part of the same system, and that they all have a role to play in maintaining nature's balance.

Stories from the Dreaming provided the foundation for the customs and beliefs of Aboriginal people, and explain the creation of natural features. Aboriginal people believe that spirits created the land, the people and other creatures. These spirits changed shape from time to time, becoming different animals, or even parts of the landscape such as granite hills or lakes.

Song lines, or Dreaming Trails, follow routes that link up special sites. For generation after generation, Aboriginal people have been taught through songs, stories, dances and their initiation that they were responsible for keeping these trails and their stories alive. Dreaming stories explain the natural features of the land.

Right: The Ochre Trail at Dryandra Woodland. Photo – Marie Lochman

RECENT TIMES

After European settlement, Aboriginal communities survived around the small towns that sprang up across the South-West. Their interconnected family groups remained the basis of their communal life as they became more urban-oriented during the twentieth century. During the Second World War, many Aboriginal people from the South-West began migrating to towns far away from their homelands to find work. The network of people with ties to the South-West spread far afield.

The Nyoongar people have preserved their identity in many ways. In some towns, local associations provide a focus for Nyoongar enterprises, and a collective voice for speaking out on issues of concern to Aboriginal people. Several groups have entered into commercial ventures, including tourism businesses, as a means of sharing their culture.

The land continues to play an important role in the life of Aboriginal people today. Associations exist with places traditionally used by Nyoongar people, places for which creation stories exist, and for places that are associated with Aboriginal life as it has adapted since European settlement. Archaeological sites, which are continually being found, have an inherent cultural significance to Aboriginal people, and also provide a means of understanding their past.

Some sites of significance to Aboriginal people are signposted and accessible to the public, such as the fish trap at Oyster Harbour near Albany. All Aboriginal sites in Western Australia are protected.

In an effort to keep the rich culture of the Nyoongar people alive, the Nyoongar Language and Culture Centre produces a range of materials including Nyoongar to English and English to Nyoongar dictionaries, video tapes with song, language and stories, and teaching materials. The centre has offices in Bunbury and Perth.

TODAY'S REMINDERS

Many place names in Western Australia's South-West are a tangible reminder of the rich culture of Aboriginal people. Many towns and sites are still known by their Aboriginal names, including Nornalup (place of the black snake), Tambellup (place of thunder), Gnowangerup (home or nest of the malleefowl), Wagin (place of the emu) and Mandurah (place of burnt trees). The use of 'in' or 'up' in the names of many towns means 'place of'.

MORE INFORMATION

It is possible to learn more about Aboriginal culture from the different Aboriginal enterprises that operate in many towns. These include tourism businesses which share the culture of Aboriginal people, art and craft outlets, and guided tours. For more information about Aboriginal enterprises, contact CALM's Aboriginal Tourism, Education and Training Unit, the Department of Aboriginal Affairs offices or local Aboriginal associations that exist in many towns.

Red Gold

The first people to live in Dryandra discovered and began mining the deep red ochre. These are their open-cut pits. Ochre is a clay that was highly prized in aboriginal culture as paint for body decoration, bark painting and rock art. High-quality ochre was often carried over great distances to be traded between different tribes. Take a pinch of ochre, mix it with saliva and see the rich, red paint as it has been used for thousands of years.

Bush Books

How can you tell a humpback from a southern right whale, a jarrah from a marri or a kestrel from a kite? It's easy when you are travelling with a set of **Bush Books**!

Bush Books are a series of practical field guides to help people discover and learn about the State's unique plants, animals and special features, region by region. More than 20 titles have been released, and more are planned.

Bush Books are pocket-sized, and each is based around a defined geographic region which contributes to their relative ease of use. The books are inexpensive, retailing for $5.95 each, and are readily available from many outlets throughout the State, including most bookshops, many newsagents, CALM offices, RAC shops, many tourist information centres and other specialist outlets, such as camping shops. All but one are in full colour.

Many regions in the State already have their own series. Titles relevant to the South-West and Goldfields include:

Common Trees of the South-West Forests
Common Trees of the Goldfields
Common Wildflowers of the South-West Forests
Orchids of the South-West
Wildflowers of the South Coast
Common Birds of the South-West Forests
Birds in the Backyard
Mammals of the South-West
Whales and Dolphins of Western Australia
Bush Tucker Plants of the South-West
Beachcomber's Guide to South-West Beaches
Australian Birds of Prey
Rare Birds of Western Australia
Bugs in the Backyard

Similar pocket-sized guides, CALM's **Discovery** books, focus on special areas, their history, local bushwalks or nature drives, attractions, plants and animals, and recreational activities. They are designed to help visitors make the most of their visit and also make great souvenirs.

Discovery books are also sold for $5.95 each. They include:

Discovering the Valley of the Giants and Walpole-Nornalup National Park
Discovering Penguin Island and the Shoalwater Islands Marine Park
Discovering Yanchep National Park

More books in both series are being released all the time, so in your travels throughout the South-West, keep your eyes posted for new titles.

CALM on the Internet

NATUREBASE

CALM's NatureBase website is a great way to find out more about the State's natural areas and how they are managed. Found at **http://www.calm.wa.gov.au**, NatureBase has 11 main subject areas. These include 'About CALM', 'Projects', 'Forest Facts', '*LANDSCOPE* Online', 'National Parks and Other Places', 'Tourism and Recreation', 'Plants and Animals', 'Science Matters', 'Latest News' and a secure online bookshop.

Viewers can browse the site, download and print information, buy books, search for specific information and send comments and e-mail. 'About CALM' gives information about the department, and lists contact details for its regional and district offices.

Under 'National Parks' you will find a region-based quick reference guide to recreation facilities in CALM-managed parks, reserves and State forest areas, as well as our regular 'Park of the Month' feature. In 'Tourism and Recreation' you can find out about many nature-based tourism activities such as *LANDSCOPE* Expeditions, Whale Watching, walking the Bibbulmun Track, and Geikie Gorge boat tours, among others. Contact details for tour operators, who are licensed to visit parks and reserves managed by CALM, are also available.

Conservation initiatives, such as *Western Shield*, can be found under the 'Projects' icon, while 'Forest Facts' gives information on the State's forest management. 'Latest News' provides a summary of CALM's news releases, together with their full text.

There is also an area specifically for schools. Here, teachers can obtain information on a wide range of educational programs and activities, and download student activity packs and resource notes. CALM's full range of publications can be ordered in the 'Bookshop' area. You can also subscribe to *LANDSCOPE* magazine and buy national park passes.

WILD ABOUT WESTERN AUSTRALIA

The Department of Conservation and Land Management has produced an interactive CD-ROM – *Wild About Western Australia* – that brings alive the natural history of WA, while taking you to all of WA's national parks and many other natural attractions.

You can learn more about WA's natural wonders, and visit even the most remote ones through this informative CD-ROM. Pictures, text, video and audio commentary enable the user to journey to Karijini, Purnululu (the Bungle Bungle), D'Entrecasteaux and Nambung national parks and to other special places such as Monkey Mia and the Tree Top Walk in the Valley of the Giants. You can even experience 'virtual reality' and enjoy all-round 360° views, or zoom in for a close-up – it's almost like being there! Colourful images of plants, and the vibrant sounds of birds and other animals, are brought to life right there on your screen.

Wild About Western Australia is for everyone who wants to learn more about the natural wonders of WA, and a trip planner is included to help visitors plan their holidays. You can call up maps and get information, such as a list of licensed commercial tourism services operating in the place of your choice. Schools and individual students will, at the touch of a button, enjoy its 'live lessons', and bushwalkers will gain a vivid insight into the terrain, animals and plants at places they wish to visit.

Whether you are planning a holiday trip, deciding where to spend weekend leisure time, want information for school projects, or just enjoy learning more about WA's plants and animals, *Wild About Western Australia* is a great resource and easy to use. Eight icons on the home page point to a variety of ways to begin sightseeing. These are:

- **Where in the West** – Choose your national park
- **Perth Outdoors** – See popular spots around Perth
- **Must See** – Visit 10 of the best places in WA
- **Snap Shots** – View great photographs of unique beauty spots
- **Out and About** – Get advice on a range of nature-based activities and find out where to go for some outdoor fun
- **About Plants** – Explore WA's wildflowers and other plants
- **Wild Things** – Meet some of our native animals
- **About CALM** – Learn about the chief agency that manages most of WA's natural treasures

Wild About Western Australia can be obtained from CD-ROM retailers and bookstores throughout Australia, as well as from CALM's State Headquarters in Dick Perry Avenue, Kensington, *WA Naturally* at 47 Henry Street (corner of Croke Street), Fremantle and some local CALM offices.

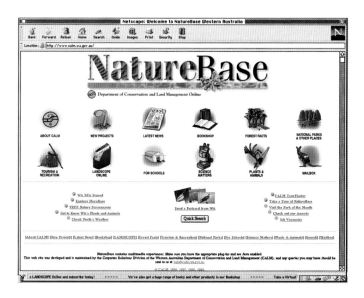

THE WOODLANDS

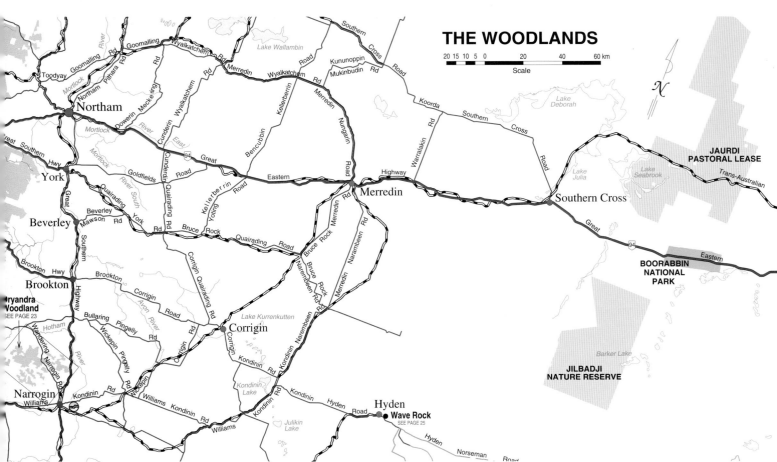

Woodlands

Narrogin to Kalgoorlie

The Wheatbelt extends from Northampton, south to Mount Barker and Jerramungup and east to Lake King. Much of the original vegetation of the region has been lost due to widespread clearing for agriculture, with about 78 per cent taken up in rural holdings. What remains can be loosely grouped into woodlands, mallee, scrub or heath.

Wandoo (*Eucalyptus wandoo*) and York gum (*E. loxophleba*) are common on the better soils in the west, while powderbark (*E. accedens*) occurs on gravelly hills. Salmon gum (*E. salmonophloia*) is most frequently found on heavy valley soils but, like other woodland species, has been extensively cleared. Mallees are found over a wide area of the Wheatbelt, particularly in the south and south-east. The open heath and mallee scrub of the Wheatbelt support a wealth of wildflowers. Developed on deep white or yellow sand, or on shallow sand over laterite, these areas are popularly known as sandplain or kwongan. The number of plant species in some small areas of the Wheatbelt is remarkable. For instance, Tutanning Nature Reserve has more than 400 plant species in an area of about 2 000 hectares.

The Goldfields, to the east, also has an interesting flora. Nowhere else in the world will one find such a diversity of tall trees in such an arid climate. Of about 500 eucalypt species in Australia, roughly 16 per cent (about 80 species) are found in the Goldfields. Of these, 34 grow only in the Goldfields, making the area very rich in endemic eucalypts. The northern third of the Goldfields is dominated by mulga (*Acacia aneura*), spinifex (*Triodia* species) and salt lake communities. The vegetation of the southern part is considered transitional between the moist south-west and the desert country, and contains species from both regions.

FACING PAGE
View from the Ochre Trail, Dryandra Forest. Photo – Marie Lochman
Below: Goldfields woodland. Photo – Jiri Lochman

Dryandra Woodland

Less than two hours from Perth, Dryandra Woodland is one of the prime places in the South-West for viewing native wildlife. Although the numbat is probably Dryandra's best known inhabitant, woylies, tammar wallabies, brushtail possums, tawny frogmouths, kangaroos and wallabies are regularly seen on night spotlighting tours. More than 100 species of bird live in the area, including the mound-building malleefowl.

Under the 'Return to Dryandra' project, which is part of CALM's *Western Shield* campaign (see page 12), a predator-proof compound containing core populations of western barred bandicoots, rufous hare-wallabies, banded hare-wallabies, boodies and bilbies, has been built to provide a safe environment for breeding. The offspring will be released into the wild in Dryandra and other CALM reserves in the South-West.

Dryandra boasts scenic woodlands and spectacular spring wildflowers. The open, graceful woodlands of white-barked wandoo and powderbark once covered much of the Wheatbelt before it was cleared for farming. Thickets of rock sheoak provide habitat for several of Dryandra's rare species, including tammar wallabies and red-tailed phascogales.

RECREATION

A series of walk and cycle trails cater for all levels of fitness, from one kilometre to 12.5 kilometres, and there is a popular radio drive trail, known as the Sounds of Dryandra Woodland. One of the most interesting walks is the Ochre Trail, which describes some of the modern and ancient Aboriginal Nyoongar culture of the Dryandra area and features an ochre pit. Ochre was used for decoration.

CALM offers *Wonders of the Woodland* at Dryandra, an activities program which provides visitors with enriching and memorable experiences based on Dryandra's natural and cultural features. These activities include night time spotlighting tours, stargazing, and traditional bushcraft with local Nyoongars. Contact the CALM Narrogin office for further details.

Accommodation is available in six self-contained restored forestry cottages (sleeping up to 12 people) with gas stoves, fridges, beds, hot water and open fireplaces, and in two smaller cottages. Up to 60 people can also be accommodated in two dormitories. You may camp at Congelin, where low impact campground facilities, bins for recycling rubbish, and gas barbecues have been installed. Other accommodation for visitors is available in the area, including farmstays.

TIMBER CUTTING HISTORY

Dryandra was originally dedicated as State forest in 1903, for protection of water catchments and timber harvesting. Sleepers were cut from wandoo, and the tannin from brown mallet bark was used to produce leather. Today,

Dryandra contains about 7 500 hectares of mallet plantations, which now provide an ideal resource for tool handle production, fence posts and firewood. Wandoo is no longer harvested.

Lookout trees once helped to protect the woodland and mallet plantations from the ravages of wildfire. One can be seen at Lol Gray and another at Congelin on the Sounds of Dryandra Woodland radio drive trail.

WHERE IS IT? 164 km south-east of Perth and 24 km north-west of Narrogin.

TRAVELLING TIME: Less than 2 hours from Perth.

TOTAL AREA: Around 28 000 ha.

WHAT TO DO: Picnicking, scenic driving, bushwalking, horse riding, cycling, night spotlighting for woodland animals, camping.

Sounds of Dryandra Drive Trail: A 25 km radio drive trail helps you to discover tales of the Nyoongar people, early forestry days, bush railways and unique wildlife. Start from the information shelter at the Old Mill Dam and head west, away from the old forestry settlement. At each signpost, stop your car and tune your radio to 100 FM.

Contine Bridle Trail: Easy 27 km, 5 hour horseriding trail from the Contine Hill picnic area.

FACILITIES: Gas barbecues, tables, toilets. Camping fees are payable.

WALKS:

Ochre Trail: Medium 5 km, 2 hour walk describes the Nyoongar culture of the Dryandra area and visits an ochre pit used for decoration.

Woylie Walk: Medium 5.5 km, 2 hour walk that begins from the Old Mill Dam picnic area.

Wandoo Walk: Easy 1 km, 30 minute walk through wandoo woodland beginning from the Old Mill Dam picnic area.

Kawana Road Walk: With luck, you'll see kangaroos, brush wallabies and malleefowl on this 8 km, 2½ hour walk which starts at the Dryandra settlement.

Lol Gray Trail: Medium 12.5 km, 4 hour return walk from the Dryandra settlement to the Lol Gray fire tower.

Lol Gray Loop: Medium to difficult 3.2 km, 1 hour loop following the old telegraph line down the hill from the Lol Gray picnic area.

NEAREST CALM OFFICE: Narrogin District Office on (08) 9881 1113. For bookings call the village caretaker on (08) 9884 5231.

Brown mallet plantation. Photo – Jiri Lochman

cenic Drive(unsealed)

ounds of Dryandra
oodland Drive Trail   1.

To Wandering 36km

To Wandering 49km

Yornaning

Road

Gura

Rd

Coolbardie Rd

Koomal

Rd

Attunga   Rd

Williams

Marri   Rd

Dryandra Settlement

Kawana

Road

Lol Gray Picnic Area

Yornaning

Road

Dryandra
Arboretum

Road

Great

Nyingarn   Rd

Tomingley

Baaluc   Rd

1.

Rd

Old Mill Dam

Dryandra   Road

Colac   Road

Wandering   Road

Cuballing

Road

West

Cuballing

Southern

Norn   Rd

6.

Fire Tower

2

andering 39km

Wandering

3.

York

Congelin Dam
Picnic Area

4.   Patonga   Rd

5

Road

Congelin
Campground

Springham   Rd

Narrogin

Rd

Siding   Rd

Contine   Rd

Highway

Williams   Rd

To Williams 28km

RYANDRA WOODLAND

0 1 2 3 4 5 km

Scale

Congelin   Rd

Narrogin   Road

Rosedale   Road

Contine Hill Picnic Area

Nebrikinning   Road

Whitford

Congelin

Narrogin   Road

Wave Rock

Wave Rock is one of the most well-known landforms in Western Australia. It rises about 15 metres above the ground like a giant wave about to break. The 'Wave' is not a separate rock, but an overhanging natural wall more than 100 metres long, on the northern side of a granite rock outcrop known as Hyden Rock.

The most likely cause of the rock's shape is the weathering of the granite below ground by water before the rock was exposed. Along its full length, it is streaked with vertical bands of rusty red, ochre and sandy grey. The vertical streaks are caused by algal growth. The dark black stains are living algae attached to the granite. They change to brown when the water supply disappears and the algae die. Algae which have been dead for a few seasons fall away from the rock, leaving fresh bare granite.

Other fascinating rock structures are also found nearby. The colourfully named Hippo's Yawn is like a giant, yawning mouth cast in solid rock. If you don't want to drive to Hippo's Yawn, you can reach it by means of a 20 minute walk around the base of Wave Rock. At the Humps, 21 kilometres from Hyden, is Mulka's Cave, a place steeped in Aboriginal history. The walls of the cave feature Aboriginal hand prints.

ABORIGINAL HISTORY

Wave Rock, Hippo's Yawn and Mulka's Cave all feature prominently in Aboriginal stories about the Dreamtime. Mulka the Terrible (Mulka-inall-ak) was a giant who could not spear any large animals because he was cross-eyed, and had taken to eating kurloongurs (children). His wife Woorlew had to help catch kurloongurs for him to eat. After a while, Woorlew wanted to save the kurloongurs from Mulka.

She quickly gathered all the kurloongurs from many different groups to hang on to her hair and body, running fast from Mulka to the spongy Wave Rock (kittah kich). She sprung very high into the sky and put the children in the Milky Way (Bibbulmun). Bibbi is the word for 'breast milk' and the Milky Way provides breast milk for the children. Some of the kurloongurs fell from her and into a cave now called bi yee kurloongur yinna, place where the spirit babies fell (known to Europeans as Hippo's Yawn).

Woorlew now tends to her fires and keeps a constant watch over all the kurloongurs along the Milky Way. She has many fireplaces to tend but her main camp is between the constellations of Orion and Taurus. She often comes down to Earth in the form of the curlew bird. On warm clear nights you can look up and see all the kurloongurs in the Milky Way. On wet windy nights you may hear the curlew crying for the lost children.

In another story, all of the tribesmen set out to fight Mulka. To do this, they had to have special powers. They armed themselves with tektites (rocks from the sky), ochre for blending, a green stone, quartz and a pearlshell. The pearlshell had special powers because it had been given its rainbow colours by the rainbow dragons (Waugals) when they disappeared into the ocean.

Mulka saw them coming and was chased to Lake Dumbleyung, where he was wounded badly. He was beheaded at Karrt-aning. Karrt means 'head' and so the town of Katanning was named. All of the parts of his body were scattered all over the land, and places were named after different belongings and different parts of his body.

Mulka's mouth (dtarr) fell at Darkan (place of mouth), his ear (dwonk) ended up at Dongara (place of ear), his backside ended up at Lake Kwonnerup. Places all around the South-West are named after different belongings, such as Kojonup (stone axe or koitch), Gidgegannup (spear or gidgie) and so on.

WHERE IS IT? Hyden is 340 km south-east of Perth and Wave Rock is 4 km east of Hyden.

TRAVELLING TIME: 4 hours from Perth.

TOTAL AREA: Wave Rock is on a 160 ha Shire reserve.

WHAT TO DO: Picnicking, scenic driving, bushwalking, horseriding, cycling.

FACILITIES: Shops, chalets, caravan park, hotel-motel in Hyden, farmstays in local area.

WALKS:

Wave Rock to Hippo's Yawn: A 20 minute walk leads around the base of Wave Rock to Hippo's Yawn.

Guided Aboriginal cultural walks are also available.

NEAREST CALM OFFICE: Narrogin District Office on (08) 9881 1113. For bookings and further information about the accommodation contact the resort manager on (08) 9880 5022. Other information can be obtained from the information centre at Wave Rock or the Wave Rock Caravan Park.

FACING PAGE
Top : Wave Rock.
Below: Hippo's Yawn. Photos – Ashley de Prazer/CALM

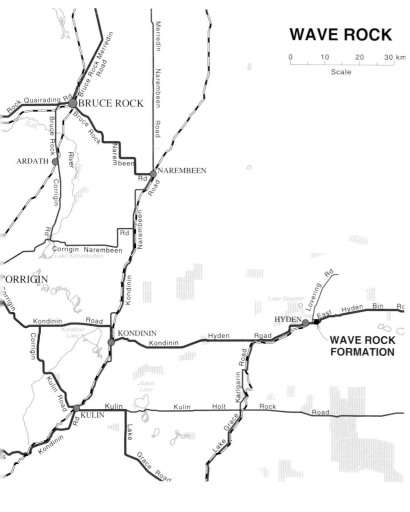

WAVE ROCK

Scale
0   10   20   30 km

BRUCE ROCK

ARDATH

NAREMBEEN

CORRIGIN

KONDININ

HYDEN

WAVE ROCK FORMATION

KULIN

Holland Track

The Holland Track provides four-wheel-drivers with an ideal opportunity to discover the woodlands of the western Goldfields. Granite outcrops, diverse eucalypt woodlands, wildflowers and the visible remains of a rich history make for a fascinating journey.

The discovery of gold in the region late last century stimulated great interest throughout Australia, and by the end of 1892 a goldrush had commenced. Many interstaters, or 't'othersiders' as they were known, arrived at Albany by ship, and travelled north to York aboard the steam trains of the Great Southern Railway. From there, it was another 450 kilometres of track to the Goldfields. This tedious journey led to the call for a more direct route.

In April 1893, Richard John Holland and his team successfully blazed a track from Broomehill, in the Wheatbelt, through to Coolgardie that would take two to three weeks off the average trip time. Holland's efforts enabled hundreds of diggers to reach the Goldfields. However, the completion of the Northam-Coolgardie rail line in 1896 saw the eventual abandonment of the route. It was not until 1993 that the eastern half of the original route, between Hyden and Coolgardie, was retraced and cleared.

Holland named many of the features along the route, including Mt Holland and Victoria Rock. His recount of the journey makes mention of '...a fine patch of sandalwood – about 30 tons...' at Sandalwood Rocks, numerous granite outcrops and claypans full of water. Although he made few references to specific wildlife, he did mention that emus were occasionally numerous and that after leaving Mt Holland the party travelled '...about twelve miles through heavy forest country, principally blackbutt, morrel and salmon gum.' Stands of such timber were to play an important role in the development of the Goldfields.

Holland's epic journey no doubt alerted the mining community to the great timber resources in the area, needed to support the thousands of kilometres of shafts and stopes under the ground. Woodland timbers were also used as fuel for the steam engines used to haul ore to the surface, as well as the massive pumps that helped to supply water from Mundaring. Specially constructed bush railways, known as woodlines, were used to haul timber from the woodlands into Kalgoorlie. The remains of the myriad of tracks and campsites can still be seen in the area around Victoria Rock (see page 32).

The regrowth woodlands are now used for an entirely different purpose. Adapted to harsh, dry conditions, Goldfields eucalypts produce unique, strong, attractive and dense timbers. These features make them suitable for many specialty uses, such as musical instruments, parquetry flooring, fine furniture, wood turning and joinery.

Although the timbers may be tough, the desert environment is quite fragile. You can help care for it by:

- using gas for cooking wherever possible;
- sticking to marked routes;
- camping at least 100 metres away from waterholes, which are often the only source of water for desert animals for many kilometres;
- taking all rubbish out with you, as foxes will dig up buried rubbish;
- avoid using the track during wet conditions to prevent damage to the track surface;
- not driving over the fragile mosses and lichens on granite outcrops;
- ensuring your car isn't carrying mud from dieback areas, as some granite outcrops in the eastern Wheatbelt have been affected this way.

HOLLAND TRACK

WHERE IS IT? The Holland Track stretches between Hyden and Coolgardie (approximately 360 km). The Holland Track Map Book (Explorer Series Western Australia: No. 1) has further details of the route and is available from CALM's *WA Naturally* outdoors information centre and RAC shops.

TRAVELLING TIME: Allow 3 days.

WHAT TO DO: Bushwalking, photography, camping.

FACILITIES: No facilities apart from campsites, barbecues and toilets at Victoria Rock. Make sure you carry plenty of water and fuel.

BEST SEASON: Autumn and spring.

FACING PAGE
Salmon gum woodland. Photo – Jiri Lochman

Rowles Lagoon Conservation Park

Rowles Lagoon Conservation Park, along with its adjacent lakes in the surrounding Clear and Muddy Lakes Nature Reserve, has been a popular recreation area for Goldfields families and other visitors for many years. The freshwater lagoon relies on rainfall to maintain its depth and, when full, it offers excellent opportunities for water-based recreation and wetland studies.

Barbecues and picnic tables are located in shaded areas around the lagoon, and toilets are also provided. As the area is a conservation park, pets are not permitted and vehicles must remain on defined tracks. A range of facilities have been developed for both day trippers and larger groups wanting extended camping weekends. Activities include birdwatching, swimming, catching yabbies and unpowered boating – when the water depth permits.

Rowles Lagoon and the surrounding lakes (Clear, Carnage and Muddy) are a birdwatcher's paradise. The lakes are environmentally significant, and are included in Australia's register of significant wetlands. A wide range of waterfowl visit the area. Black swans, pink-eared ducks and wood ducks are commonly found, along with several rare species, including the freckled duck, which is Australia's rarest waterbird. Dedicated birdwatchers may wish to pick up a pamphlet listing all birds recorded at Rowles Lagoon from CALM's Kalgoorlie office.

Rowles Lagoon can be included in an interesting day circuit visit to the gold mining ghost towns of Broad Arrow and Ora Banda, and to Coolgardie. Each ghost town has a hotel with picnic and barbecue facilities. The Ora Banda Hotel, built of stone from the original open cut gold mine nearby, had fallen into disrepair, but was refurbished between 1981 and 1985 and the historic inn now does a roaring trade. The hotel at Broad Arrow, with its original tin roof and walls, has continued to trade non-stop since the headier gold-mining days of the 1890s. Both are set amid the disarray of the history-laden ruins of former mining camps.

WHERE IS IT? 73 km north of Coolgardie along the Bonnie Vale and Carbine Roads.

TRAVELLING TIME: 1 hour from Coolgardie.

TOTAL AREA: Rowles Lagoon Conservation Park is 404 ha; the surrounding nature reserves are 1 926 ha.

WHAT TO DO: Walking, birdwatching, swimming, yabby fishing, canoeing, picnicking, camping.

FACILITIES: Tables, barbecues, toilets, camping sites, boat launching site.

NEAREST CALM OFFICE:
The Kalgoorlie Regional Office is at the Post Office Public Building in Hannan Street, Kalgoorlie, phone (08) 9021 2677.

ROWLES LAGOON CONSERVATION PARK

FACING PAGE
Top: Rowles Lagoon. Photo – Marie Lochman
Below: Ora Banda Hotel. Photo – Dennis Sarson/Lochman Transparencies

Kalgoorlie

Kalgoorlie-Boulder is the gold capital of Australia. Kalgoorlie's days of glory began in 1893, when Paddy Hannan and his fellow Irish prospectors, Thomas Flanagan and Dan Shea, found gold near Mt Charlotte. Other prospectors soon discovered the immense deposits of the Golden Mile, reputed to be the richest square mile of gold-bearing earth in the world, and before long thousands of men from all ends of the globe had set up camp in the area.

The major problem holding back the region, the lack of water, was solved in 1903, with the completion of a 563 kilometre water pipeline from Mundaring Weir, near Perth, designed by engineer C Y O'Connor.

Kalgoorlie boasts a number of unique attractions. You can take underground tours of the Hannans North Mine and witness the life of miners at the turn of the century. For safety reasons, enclosed shoes must be worn underground. On the surface, ride the railway around the seven hectare site. Watch the unique method of refining gold in the Gold Pour demonstration and try your luck panning for gold. For a view of modern day operations, go to the Golden Mile Super Pit Lookout, off the Eastern Bypass Road, to view the massive open cut mine.

Paddy Hannans Tree, in Outridge Terrace, marks the site where Hannan, Flanagan and Shea discovered gold while riding through the area in 1893. Another relic of Kalgoorlie's colourful past is the original and only Bush Two-Up, a corrugated iron structure where thousands of dollars change hands on the toss of the pennies.

The entrance to the Museum of the Goldfields is formed by the Ivanhoe Headframe, the second largest headframe from the famous Golden Mile. A glass-sided lift takes visitors to the viewing platform for a bird's eye view of the city and mines. Gold and sandalwood are two of the main themes of an impressive range of exhibits and 'hands on' activities. These include an underground vault containing specimens from the State Gold Collection and an outdoor sandalwood camp. The approach is also remarkable for the ethnobotanical gardens on either side, which exhibit native plants, their Aboriginal names and traditional uses.

Once the busiest station in Western Australia, the Loopline Railway was the major form of transport for miners at the turn of the century. Today visitors can ride the 'Rattler' for an hour-long commentated journey around the Golden Mile.

KALGOORLIE ARBORETUM

A wide variety of local eucalypts, walktrails for all ages, picnic tables under the shade of river gums and a small dam that attracts waterbirds are some of the features of the Kalgoorlie Arboretum. It is a great place for a picnic and to learn more about the trees of the Goldfields.

The arboretum, set on 26 hectares of land at Hawkins Street adjacent to Hammond Park, is just five minutes from central Kalgoorlie. It was established in 1954 by the former Forests Department to test and demonstrate the suitability of native and exotic trees to the semi-arid environment of the Goldfields. Since then, seed from these tree species has been exported to similar semi-arid countries around the world. About 60 eucalypt species have been planted in the last 40 years.

A major upgrade of visitor facilities, to cater for increasing visitor numbers, will be completed by 1999. This 'Kalgoorlie Arboretum Community Action Project' has been sponsored by Kanowna Belle Gold Mines, North Limited and The Landcare Foundation.

WHERE IS IT? 595 km east of Perth. There are also daily links from Perth to Kalgoorlie by air, train and coach.

TRAVELLING TIME: 7 hours drive from Perth.

WHAT TO DO: Walking, picnicking, scenic flights and helicopter rides, wildflower viewing (July to October) after good rains, riding the Loopline train, mine touring, visiting the Bush Two-Up, ghost town touring.

FACILITIES: Full range of accommodation and entertainment facilities. The Kalgoorlie Arboretum has tables, toilets, a catchment dam, a grassed shady picnic area and walktrails.

NEAREST CALM OFFICE: The Kalgoorlie Regional Office is at the Post Office Public Building in Hannan Street, Kalgoorlie, phone (08) 9021 2677.

FACING PAGE
Top left: Cassidy Shaft, Tower Gold Mine. Photo – John Kleczkowski
Top right: Historic Federal Hotel in Kalgoorlie. Photo – Dennis Sarson
Below: The 'Rattler' on the Golden Mile Loopline train journey. Photo – Dennis Sarson
All photos on p.30-31 supplied by Lochman Transparencies
Gold bars from the WA Mint. Photo – Len Stewart

Coolgardie nature reserves

VICTORIA ROCK

One of the most spectacular granite outcrops in the Goldfields can be seen at Victoria Rock Nature Reserve. The magnificent regrowth woodland around the rock consists of salmon gum, gimlet and redwood. Closer to the rock, thickets of rock sheoak provide an ideal spot for picnickers and campers. Nestled beside the rock are numerous secluded sites, complete with bush furniture, barbecues and toilets to cater for visitors and campers.

BURRA ROCK

Burra Rock Nature Reserve contains several large granite rocks surrounded by regrowth woodland. It also has a dam and catchment wall that supplied water for steam-driven engines on the narrow-gauge railways (woodlines) bringing timber to Kalgoorlie-Boulder in the late 1920s. The regrowth woodland around Burra Rock is the result of clearfelling in 1927 to supply fuel wood for steam-driven engines and structural timber for the gold mining industry.

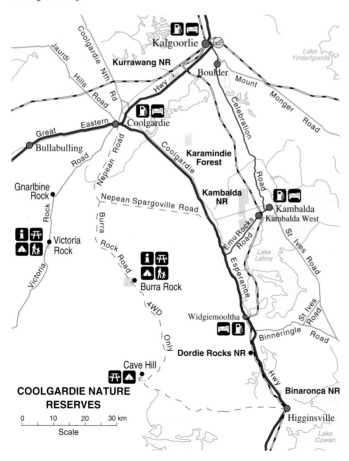

At Burra Rock Dam, visitors are assured of a great view and a feed of yabbies. Nature study and exploring the rock are other popular activities. The view from the summit stretches for as far as the eye can see, over the regenerated woodlands.

CAVE HILL

For those with four-wheel-drive vehicles, a trip along the woodline towards Cave Hill can be a memorable and historically interesting experience. There are a number of old woodline camps along this trail.

Cave Hill Nature Reserve is an excellent camping spot and is also suitable for longer day trips from Kalgoorlie-Boulder or Coolgardie. The reserve is dominated by a spectacular granite outcrop, with a large cave formation on the western side, which gives the rock its name. The rock also acts as a catchment for a number of dams. The surrounding woodland offers pleasant sites for picnics, walks and wildlife.

Visitors are urged not to drive off tracks or on the rocks, as the fragile granite and other historical features are easily damaged. Pets are not permitted in any nature reserve.

WHERE ARE THEY? Victoria Rock Nature Reserve is 43 km south of Coolgardie on the Victoria Rock Road. Burra Rock Nature Reserve is 60 km south of Coolgardie, past the old Nepean Mine on the Burra Rock Road. Cave Hill Nature Reserve is 60 km west of Higginsville off the Coolgardie-Esperance Highway (dry weather access only and 4WD only from Burra Rock).

TRAVELLING TIME: 30 minutes (Victoria Rock), 45 minutes (Burra Rock) or 3 hours (Cave Hill) from Coolgardie.

TOTAL AREA: Victoria Rock Nature Reserve is 258 ha, Burra Rock Nature Reserve is 809 ha and Cave Hill Nature Reserve is 202 ha.

WHAT TO DO: Camping, yabby fishing, picnicking, walking.

FACILITIES: All three reserves have campsites, picnic tables, barbecue rings and toilets.

NEAREST CALM OFFICE: The Kalgoorlie Regional Office is at the Post Office Public Building in Hannan Street, Kalgoorlie, phone (08) 9021 2677.

FACING PAGE
Top: Victoria Rock. Photo – Dennis Sarson/Lochman Transparencies
Below: Bobtail skink. Photo – Jiri Lochman

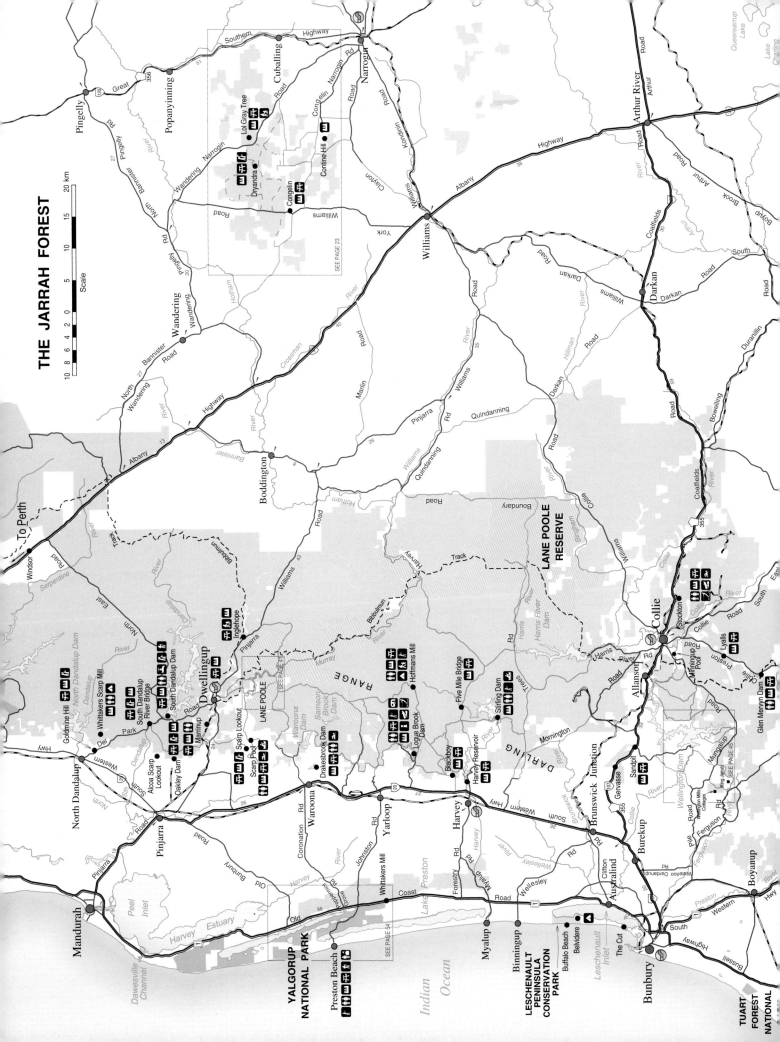

THE JARRAH FOREST

Scale
20 km
15
10
5
2
0
10 8 6 4 2 0

To Perth

Mandurah

Pinjarra

North Dandalup

Goldmine Hill

Whittakers Scarp Mill

South Dandalup River Bridge

South Dandalup Dam

Alcoa Scarp Lookout

Oakley Dam

Marrinup

Dwellingup

Scarp Lookout

Scarp Pool

Drakesbrook Dam

Waroona

Yarloop

Harvey Reservoir

Harvey

Blackboy

Five Mile Bridge

Logue Brook Dam

Samson Brook Dam

Waroona Dam

Stirling Dam

Hoffmans Mill

Inglehope

Pinjarra

Boddington

Wandering

Popanyinning

Pingelly

Narrogin

Cuballing

Contine Hill

Dryandra

Congelin

Lol Gray Tree

Williams

Darkan

Arthur River

Collie

Stockton

Allanson

Brunswick Junction

Burekup

Australind

Clifton

Myalup

Binningup

Buffalo Beach

Belvidere

The Cut

Bunbury

Boyanup

Mornington

Gervasse

Sandpit

Wellington Mills Cottages

Glen Mervyn Dam

Mungalup

Lyalls

Minningup Pool

LANE POOLE RESERVE

DARLING RANGE

YALGORUP NATIONAL PARK

Preston Beach

LESCHENAULT PENINSULA CONSERVATION PARK

TUART FOREST NATIONAL

Peel Inlet

Harvey Estuary

Dawesville Channel

Lake Preston

Indian Ocean

Leschenault Inlet

Wellington Dam

SEE PAGE 23

SEE PAGE 41

SEE PAGE 54

SEE PAGE 45

The Jarrah Forests

Dwellingup to Collie

Tall green forest that overlooks deep river valleys, spring wildflowers and ancient granite outcrops that rise above the tops of trees are all features of the jarrah forest between Dwellingup and Collie.

The parks and reserves of the Darling Range offer a host of different places to find, whether you're looking for somewhere to escape to for a week, or somewhere new to visit on a day trip. In the forest there are places to camp, walk and picnic. There are long rivers to canoe, small creeks to explore, dams to fish and the ghosts of old mill towns to investigate.

THE JARRAH FOREST

The Darling Range is ancient. This range of low hills, which back the eastern edge of the Swan Coastal Plain from near Moora to Busselton, supports an intriguing and complex community of plants and animals called the jarrah forest.

The western edge of the range catches the moisture-laden onshore winds and forces them up to dump their load of rain. Dwellingup, in the heart of the tall western jarrah forest, receives an average of about 1 500 millimetres of rain each year. Mandurah, less than 40 kilometres to the west, and down on the coastal plain, receives about half of this.

The deeply eroded valleys of the range contain the richest and the deepest soils, but there are few permanent streams or rivers. The jarrah trees, which dominate the forest of the Darling Range, grow fastest and largest in these areas. Marri is the second most common forest tree, and often grows with jarrah. Blackbutt is frequently found in moist, fertile valleys. In swampy areas, the pale silvery barked bullich forms small stands, and on sites that overlie clay, particularly near the western and eastern perimeters of the Darling Plateau, wandoo often becomes the main forest tree.

Jarrah forest. Photo – Dennis Sarson/Lochman Transparencies

Dwellingup

Dwellingup is the gateway to the jarrah and marri forest that clothes the hilly country surrounding the Murray River. Tranquil river streams, swelling to fast-moving rapids in winter, fill the Murray River valley. Paperbarks, flooded gums and blackbutt fringe the river. Away from the water, the hilly terrain is covered with beautiful jarrah forest.

HISTORY

Dwellingup was first settled in 1910, and rapidly became the centre of a booming timber industry. Timber cutters from a network of mills such as Holyoake, Marrinup and Chadoora worked the forest nearby, producing jarrah sleepers and other timber products for export, which were then taken by rail to the docks at Rockingham. By 1918, the jarrah forest was dedicated as State forest by an Act of Parliament, and Dwellingup became a base for forest management, and later for research.

During the Second World War, a Prisoner of War camp for German and Italian prisoners was established at Marrinup, a few kilometres north-west of Dwellingup. The camp took its first prisoners in August 1943 and released the last in April 1946. It was built to accommodate 1 600 men, who were set to work labouring on farms and cutting firewood. Thousands of prisoners passed through its gates. Most were Italian and German, who were put in separate compounds in accordance with the Geneva Convention. The old camp is one stop on a self-guided 16 kilometre drive tour through the forest. The Marrinup Forest Tour Guide, available from the local CALM office, explains the features of this fascinating scenic drive.

In January 1961, fierce bushfires started by lightning devastated the area, damaging tens of thousands of hectares of forest and destroying most of the small mill towns nearby. It destroyed homes, settlements and bush railways but, amazingly, there was no loss of life. Dwellingup is the only town that was rebuilt. It is now home to 350 or so residents. Most of them live and work in the forest, maintaining the town's ties with the attractive jarrah that surrounds it.

RECREATION

Nearby recreation areas feature tall shady jarrah and marri forest, views from the edge of the scarp over the coastal plain, small streams and large dams. North and South Dandalup dams offer breathtaking views and picnic areas. There is also a landscaped recreation site and swimming area below the dam wall of North Dandalup. Both dams supply fresh water to the people of the South-West, so boating, fishing and marroning is not allowed. Oakley Dam, on the western edge of the Darling Scarp, is stocked with rainbow trout and redfin perch and offers recreational fishing opportunities. It has barbecues and picnic tables, and overlooks the Alcoa Alumina Refinery and the coastal plain.

White water rafting is also a popular activity. From about mid-June to mid-October you can pit yourself against a wild river, as the Murray River makes its thrilling descent down the Darling Scarp. The river is graded between three and four, depending on the water level and velocity. The wildest river that can be commercially rafted is graded at five, so it is extremely challenging.

The 40.6 kilometre long Murray River is also suitable for canoeing, depending on the season. Informative guides for canoeing the Murray River are available from tourist information centres in the area. Get together a group of three or more and plan a route, pack all necessary gear and enough food. Always allow for a change in weather and dress accordingly. Pack plenty of water too.

WHERE IS IT? 100 km south of Perth, 24 km east of Pinjarra. Recreation areas are scattered through the forest in about a 30 km radius of Dwellingup.

TRAVELLING TIME: About 1½ hours from Perth, 1 hour from Bunbury.

WHAT TO DO: White water rafting, canoeing, camping, picnicking, fishing, waterskiing, bushwalking, visiting the Forest Heritage Centre (see page 38).

Etmilyn Tramway Trail: 12 km, 1½ hour railway journey from Dwellingup Station along the Holyoake Brook valley past old and modern timber mills and bush tramways. Check details and times with the Hotham Valley Tourist Railway.

WALKS:

Marrinup Falls: Easy 1.5 km, 45 minute loop along Marrinup Brook to the Falls, returning on the opposite bank.

Cage in the Bush Walktrail: Moderate 4.5 km, 2 hour walktrail from the old Marrinup Townsite, a few kilometres north-west of Dwellingup, to the site of a former POW camp.

FACILITIES: The town is fully serviced.

NEAREST CALM OFFICE: Dwellingup District Office, Banksiadale Road, Dwellingup, phone (08) 9538 1078.

FACING PAGE
Oakley Falls. Photo – Marie Lochman

Forest Heritage Centre

The Forest Heritage Centre is a unique leaf-shaped building, set in the jarrah forest at the town of Dwellingup. Inside, you will discover Western Australia's only specialist woodworking school where visitors can meet designers and furniture makers at work, enjoy displays and exhibits which bring the forest to life, and enjoy a superb gallery featuring fine wood pieces crafted by some of Western Australia's most talented designers.

Outside, visitors can walk among the tops of trees on the forest canopy walk, wander along forest trails, or explore a traditional Aboriginal mia mia (shelter) and early timber getter's hut.

Built of rammed earth, the three leaf-shaped areas of the Forest Heritage Centre each house a different aspect of forest heritage. The largest, central leaf is home to The School of Wood – a woodworking school and work space for visiting artists-in-residence. The smaller, western leaf houses the Forest Heritage Gallery, which showcases fine wood products and forest-inspired arts and crafts. Most of these items are available for purchase. The third leaf features displays which tell the story of the forest and help visitors to understand its diversity and management.

The Forest Heritage Centre is open from 10 am to 5 pm every day and there is a charge to enter. Guided tours are available. The centre offers a range of day and weekend workshops in woodwork, with some of Western Australia's finest craftspeople, or can arrange special activities for groups of all sizes. Forest guides can take visitors to a nearby working timber mill, or stoke up the fire as they enjoy billy tea and damper in the open air.

No forest experience is complete without the joy of waking up to the sounds of the forest. The Jarrah Forest Lodge at the Forest Heritage Centre offers comfortable accommodation at budget prices. Facilities are shared. Bring your own food and linen.

WHERE IS IT? 100 km south of Perth, 24 km east of Pinjarra.

TRAVELLING TIME: About 1½ hours from Perth, 1 hour from Bunbury.

WHAT TO DO: Walking, learning about wood, meeting artisans and designers.

WALKS:

Canopy Walk: Takes visitors into the tree tops for an aerial perspective on the forest system and a bird's eye view of the craftspeople at work in the School of Wood.

Heritage Centre Walk: Fully wheelchair accessible 400 m walk. Starting from the eastern leaf, a rammed earth wall depicts the soil structure of the forest and the complex root system of the trees.

Bidi Yanna Djaril-Mari Trail: Easy 700 m walk looking at Nyoongar relationships with this forest. Collect a message stick to guide you on this path.

Timber Getters Trail: Easy 700 m loop to a reconstructed sleeper getter's camp.

FACILITIES: Fine Wood Gallery, School of Wood, tea and coffee, budget accommodation.

FURTHER ENQUIRIES AND BOOKINGS: Forest Heritage Centre, Acacia Street, Dwellingup, phone (08) 9538 1395, fax (08) 9538 1352.

FACING PAGE
Forest Canopy Walk, Forest Heritage Centre. Photo – Barbara Giles/CALM

Below left: Fine wood artist at work. Photo – Chris Garnett
Below: Forest Heritage Centre. Photo – Jiri Lochman

Lane Poole Reserve

Tall jarrah forest, steeply sloping valleys, rocky pools and the Murray River are the chief attractions of this popular reserve, 100 km south of Perth.

Running through an ancient valley of the Darling Scarp, the river forms rapids, small waterfalls and deep still pools. In winter, it can be a raging torrent, and in summer a limpid stream to swim, canoe or fish in, or just to watch and appreciate its tranquillity. In spring, the forest fills with wildflowers.

Popular camping spots include the site of the old jarrah mill at Nanga, burnt in the Dwellingup fires of 1961, and now sheltered by a grove of tall pines. Nearby, Nanga Brook flows down a trout ladder and into the Murray River. A camp primarily for schoolchildren has been established at Icy Creek near Nanga.

WHERE IS IT? 100 km south of Perth, just south of Dwellingup.

TRAVELLING TIME: About 1½ hours from Perth, 1 hour from Bunbury.

TOTAL AREA: 52 000 ha.

WHAT TO DO: White water rafting, canoeing, camping (book with the local ranger), bushwalking, swimming, picnicking.

WALKS:

King Jarrah Track: This 18 km track begins from Nanga Mill and runs along the river's edge and through jarrah forest to an ancient king jarrah.

Nanga Circuit: Moderate, 17 km, 5½ hour loop beginning and ending at Nanga Mill campsite.

Island Pool Walktrail: Moderate, 1.5 km, 45 minute loop up the side of the Murray Valley through jarrah forest and along the river, returning to Island Pool.

FACILITIES:

Baden-Powell: Separate camping and day use areas. Barbecues, shaded tables, toilets, canoe launch.

Charlies Flat: Secluded tent sites, each with a fireplace and table. Toilets.

Island Pool: Day use only. Barbecues, tables, toilets, walktrail, lookout, picnic area.

Nanga Mill: Campsites and caravan sites, barbecues, tables, toilets, firewood, children's adventure trail.

Scarp Lookout: Day use. Tables, barbecues, lookout.

Scarp Pool: Day use. Barbecues, tables, toilets, canoe launch.

Stringers: Barbecues, tables, toilets, canoe launch, walktrail.

Tonys Bend: Tent sites, each with a fireplace and table. Toilets.

NEAREST CALM OFFICE: Call in to CALM's Dwellingup office at Banksiadale Road for up-to-the-minute advice on road conditions, fire hazards and other useful information. Phone (08) 9538 1078.

FACING PAGE
Children viewing marron at Lane Poole Reserve. Photo – Jiri Lochman

Canoe convoy on the Murray River. Photo – Dennis Sarson/Lochman Transparencies

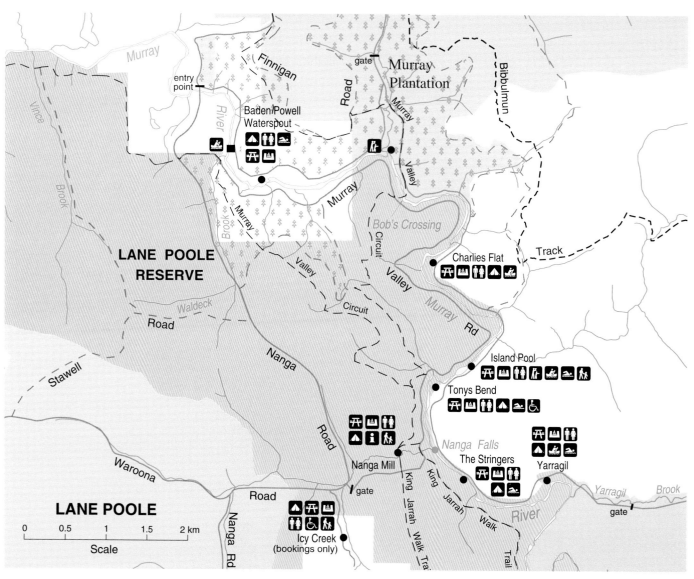

LANE POOLE RESERVE

Murray

Finnigan

gate

Murray
Plantation

entry
point

Baden Powell
Waterspout

Bibbulmun

River

Murray
Road

Murray
Valley

Vince

LANE POOLE
RESERVE

Brook

Murray
Brook

Murray

Bob's Crossing

Valley

Track

Charlies Flat

Circuit

Valley

Waldeck

Circuit

Murray
Rd

Road

Island Pool

Nanga

Tonys Bend

Stawell

Road

Nanga Falls

The Stringers

Yarragil

Waroona

Nanga Mill

gate

King
Jarrah

King
Jarrah
Walk

Yarragil
Brook

LANE POOLE

Road

River

gate

Nanga
Rd

Icy Creek
(bookings only)

Walk

Trail

| 0 | 0.5 | 1 | 1.5 | 2 km |

Scale

Harvey

Just a short distance from Perth, the State forests and other natural attractions between Harvey and Bunbury are often overlooked. They feature tall green jarrah forest on the sides of deep river valleys, spring wildflowers and ancient granite outcrops. In the forest there are places to camp, walk and picnic, long rivers to canoe, small creeks to explore, dams to fish and old mill towns to find and investigate. They offer somewhere to escape for a week or good destinations for day trips.

Like much of the northern jarrah forest, the jarrah here was logged and regenerated from the turn of the century onwards. The era left its traces. Wooden tramlines, used to run timber back to the main mill from outlying felling areas, can sometimes be discovered in the undergrowth. Stumps about two metres high are all that is left of many of the huge old jarrah trees that were felled by hand with crosscut saw and axe. Axemen used to 'high stump' to avoid having to cut the extra distances through the great buttressed trunk of the larger jarrah trees. New forests have regrown to replace the original stands.

HOFFMAN CAMPSITE

The old mill town of Hoffman is set within attractive jarrah forest on the banks of the upper reaches of the Harvey River. There are forest wildflowers in spring. The 10 hectare campground at Hoffman Mill (which has shady camping areas, water supply, toilets, and two-wheel-drive and caravan access) can accommodate a large number of campers.

Exotic flowers and fruit trees serve as a reminder of the old town. There is also a short walktrail with information panels on the area's history. Two mills were built on this site. The first, operating from 1919 to 1930, was destroyed by fire. The second, built in 1924, was the first mill in WA to use a horizontal band saw to break down the logs. On the site of the old mill itself, there are several small stands of smooth-barked eastern states gum trees. These were planted as trial plots used to test various species for their suitability to WA conditions.

DAMS

The irrigation dams of Logue Brook and Waroona, set in State forest within the Darling Range, are close to Harvey. They offer trout fishing and marroning in season, to while away a pleasant evening, and at Logue Brook and Waroona a fully serviced caravan park provides the comforts of home, including hot showers.

Waroona and Logue Brook also have a waterski area marked by buoys, complete with boat ramp.

WHERE IS IT? The town of Harvey is 140 km south of Perth via the South-West Highway. Forest recreation areas are within a 30 km radius of the town.

TRAVELLING TIME: Less than 2 hours from Perth, 40 minutes from Bunbury.

TOTAL AREA: 52 000 ha.

WHAT TO DO: Canoeing, bushwalking, swimming, picnicking, boating, waterskiing, camping.

WALKS:

Bridges Trail: Easy 3 km, 1 hour walk takes you from the trailhead sign at Hoffman Mill over the Harvey River and through jarrah forest.

Formation Trail: A short informative walk around Hoffman Mill, as it was in the bygone days.

Blackboy Trail: Easy 1.4 km, 30 minute walk just off Honeymoon Road, north of Harvey. Enjoy views of the Harvey Weir and the coastal plain.

FACILITIES: Toilets, barbecues, tables.

NEAREST CALM OFFICE: Call in to CALM's Harvey Office at 64 Weir Road for up-to-the-minute advice on road conditions, fire hazards and other useful information. Phone (08) 9729 1505.

FACING PAGE
Trout ladder on the Harvey River. Photo – Jiri Lochman

Collie

The hilly area, clothed with attractive jarrah and pine forests, that surrounds the coal mining town of Collie is wonderfully scenic. Forests, rivers and lakes provide a variety of natural settings for outdoor pursuits.

WELLINGTON FOREST AND DAM

Lush jarrah forest surrounds the spectacular Wellington Dam in the Darling Range. September to November is ideal for picnicking or bushwalking, while November to February is great for camping, swimming or canoeing the Collie River. July to September is the best time to see the rapids, and in August and September the dam may overflow.

At the dam wall there are lookouts and walking paths. Potters Gorge is a popular picnic area on the banks of the dam, with quality facilities and universal access. It features beautiful regrowth jarrah forest. The dam itself has wide expanses of water suitable for non-powered sailing craft, canoes or row boats. There is a boat launching area on Tom Jones Drive.

Gravel forest roads suitable for two-wheel-drive vehicles wind along the valley to a number of attractive picnic and camping areas on the banks of the Collie River. It is an area of great beauty, known for its wide deep pools, rapids and massive rock outcrops. Marroning and fishing (under license), canoeing, bushwalking, camping, picnicking and sightseeing are popular pursuits. The waters contain redfin perch and rainbow trout.

Honeymoon Pool is a beautiful camping and picnicking area set in lush, green jarrah forest on the banks of the Collie River. Bushwalking, fishing,

canoeing and swimming are also popular at this spot. There are separate family and group camping facilities. At night, campers share the area with friendly bandicoots and chuditch.

Wellington Mills cottages are in the Wellington Forest. The eight cottages have kitchen and bathroom amenities, a balcony and a wood burning fire. The grounds have barbecues, a playground and volleyball facilities for families and groups. The wooden cottages are available for visitors to stay in. For bookings phone (08) 9527 1844.

WELLINGTON DISCOVERY FOREST

The Wellington Discovery Forest is located in beautiful jarrah forest, about 20 kilometres east of Bunbury and 18 kilometres west of Collie. It covers 650 hectares of 100 year old, high quality regrowth forest intermixed with old growth veteran trees.

At the Wellington Discovery Forest, you can enjoy a fascinating journey into the diverse ecosystem of a jarrah forest. There are two walktrails well worth exploring. A 1.5 kilometre Jarrah Trail allows you to discover how the jarrah forest thrives in infertile soils, supports a high proportion of plants found nowhere else, survives threats from fire, drought and insects and supports five eucalypt species that you can identify. The Total Forest Trail allows you to discover how forest managers provide and protect animal homes, meet our needs for timber, provide for the creation of a new jarrah forest and protect water quality.

As further development takes place over time, the Discovery Forest will also provide the chance to climb and view the forest and surrounds from a purpose built lookout tower, to participate in guided activities, to view inspiring forest sculptures and, in the longer term, to step back in time to experience the life of a timber cutter living in the forest 90 years ago.

OTHER RECREATION SITES

About 20 kilometres north of Collie, along the Collie-Tallanalla Road, is the Harris Dam picnic site, a delightful spot with barbecues, tables, sections of boardwalk and toilets. You can walk across the dam wall to view the overflow during winter, and then walk through the parks and gardens to the picnic area.

To the east of the town, the old Stockton open cut mine has filled with water, and forms an artificial lake at the centre of a pleasant picnic area. A boat ramp, waterski and swimming areas are provided.

Wellington Dam at low water levels. Photo – Len Stewart/Lochman Transparencies

WHERE IS IT? Collie is 57 km from Bunbury and 202 km south of Perth via the South West Highway and Coalfields Highway (turn off near Roelands). The Wellington Dam Road turns off south from Coalfields Highway about 20 km from the South-West Highway.

TRAVELLING TIME: 40 minutes from Bunbury, 2½ hours from Perth.

WHAT TO DO: Swimming, bushwalking, camping, fishing.

FACILITIES: Toilets, barbecues, tables, camping areas.

WALKS:

Jarrah Trail: Easy 1.1 km, 1 hour return walk to discover the natural processes, relationships and special features that sustain the jarrah forest community.

Total Forest Trail: This 2 hour return walk explores the complex craft of managing the forest for the diverse values it provides.

Sika Circuit: Medium 9.4 km, 4 hour circuit through mature jarrah and blackbutt forest, overlooking the Collie River valley. The track follows the river for part of the way, passing rock outcrops, deep pools and several rapids, and is steep.

Harris Dam, Bibbulmun Track: Medium 8 km, 3-4 hour return walk through attractive jarrah forest from Harris Dam picnic site, north of Collie, to a timber shelter built for long-distance walkers on the Bibbulmun Track. The trail features views over the dam.

NEAREST CALM OFFICE: Mornington District Office, 147 Wittenoom Street, Collie, phone (08) 9734 1988.

Right: The Collie River in the Darling Range. Photo – Marie Lochman
Below: Camping in Wellington Forest. Photo – Gordon Roberts

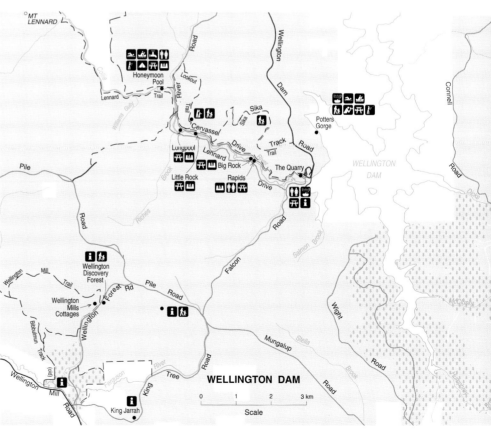

WELLINGTON DAM

THE LIMESTONE COAST

20 16 12 8 4 0   10   20   30   40 km

Scale

Indian   Ocean

Rockingham

Penguin Island

SHOALWATER ISLANDS MARINE PARK

Langford Park

Perth
Gleheagle

Jarrahdale
Eco-experience

Gooralong

Jarrahdale

Mundlimup

Serpentine

SERPENTINE NP

Balmoral
Sullivan
Rock

Albany

Windsor

Mandurah

North Dandalup

North Dandalup Dam
Dandalup

Pinjarra 19

Peel Inlet

Dawesville Channel

South Dandalup
River Bridge

South Dandalup Dam

Pinjarra

Dwellingup

YALGORUP NATIONAL PARK

Scarp Pool

Coronation Rd

Bibbulmun

Pinjarra

Waroona Dam

Waroona

Drakesbrook Dam

Preston Beach

Whittakers Mill

Yarloop

Logue Brook
Dam

Hoffmans Mill

Lake Preston

Forestry Rd Harvey

Harvey

Quindanning

Track

Indian   Ocean

Myalup

Stirling Dam

Trees

Rd

Binningup

Harris River
Dam

Harris River

LANE PO... RESER...

LESCHENAULT PENINSULA CONSERVATION PARK

Leschenault Inlet

Clifton Rd

Brunswick Junction

355 Gervasse

Australind

Collie

Bunbury

Burekup

Collie

Stockton

Wellington Dam

Boyanup

Glen Mervyn Dam

TUART FOREST NATIONAL PARK

Capel

Donnybrook

Donnybrook Boyup Brook Road

Bibbulmun

Boyup

Cape Naturaliste
Gull Rock Bunker Bay

Geographe Bay

Simpson Ludlow
River

Membenup
Layman

Dunsborough

Busselton

Kirup

Balingup

LEEUWIN-NATURALISTE NATIONAL PARK

Yallingup

Caves Rd 250

Boyup Broo...
Roa...

Cape Clairault

Wildwood Rd

Bussell Highway

Vasse

SEE PAGE 78

Moses Rock

Cowaramup

Canebrake Pool

Margaret River

Grimwade Wilga Rd

Bridgetown

Cowaramup Bay

Gracetown

Osmington Rd

Mowen Road

Nannup

Brockman

Bridgetown Jarrah Park

Indian

Kilcarnup Beach
Cape Mentelle
Prevelly Park

Margaret River

Sues

Karri Gully

Ocean

Redgate

Witchcliffe

Sues Bridge

Bobs Hollow

LEEUWIN-NATURALISTE NATIONAL PARK

Hut Pool

Brockman

Canebreak

Boranup Forest

Hamelin Bay

SCOTT NP

Twinems Bend

Manjimup

Cosy Corner

Scott River

Augusta
Flinders Bay

GINGILUP SWAMPS NATURE RESERVE

Coast Rd

South Coast Rd

Milyeannup

Fouracres

Road

Lake Quitjup
Lake Jasper

Cape Leeuwin

SEE PAGE 67

D'ENTRECASTEAUX NATIONAL PARK

Pemberton

Southern   Ocean

The Limestone Coast

Rockingham to Augusta

The limestone coast between Rockingham and Busselton is dominated by stately tuart trees, with their lush understorey of peppermints.

Near Busselton lies the Tuart Forest National Park, the last remaining pure tuart forest in the State. Next to the park, the shores of the Vasse-Wonnerup Estuary on the coast provide a haven for waterbirds. These wetlands are of international significance.

The rugged coast that runs between Cape Naturaliste and Cape Leeuwin has long been a popular holiday destination. Long beaches and sheltered bays, good fishing, superb surfing and dramatic coastal cliffs fronting the cool waters of the Indian Ocean all combine to give the area its character. Inland, the region is becoming famous for excellent wines.

Leeuwin-Naturaliste National Park, running along this coast from Bunker Bay to Augusta, protects around 15 500 hectares of rocky coastline, caves, coastal heathlands, jarrah, banksia and melaleuca woodlands, and swamps. Boranup Forest is steeped in the majesty and atmosphere of karri, the world's third tallest tree, and Augusta on the South Coast brings you more quiet bays, rugged sea cliffs and the history of one of WA's earliest settled areas.

Major towns such as Busselton, Margaret River and Augusta are within easy driving distance of all the reserves in this area. Once off the major highways, roads are usually gravel, and suitable for two-wheel-drive vehicles, but some places are only accessible by four-wheel-drive. Consult the map for each entry.

Limestone feature at Penguin Island. Photo – Michael James/CALM

Penguin Island

Penguin Island is a truly unique place. Only 42 kilometres from the centre of Perth, it is home to a diverse array of wildlife and boasts breathtaking marine and coastal scenery. It is home to the largest colony of little penguins on the west coast and probably Western Australia. The small 12.5 hectare island is less than 700 metres offshore from the growing regional centre of Rockingham. A ferry service operates between the island and the mainland.

The island and the surrounding waters of the Shoalwater Islands Marine Park provide visitors with a variety of recreational opportunities. The island has something special for visitors of all ages, whether from the local or Perth metropolitan area, interstate or overseas. Visitors can enjoy picnic areas, lookouts, pristine beaches and the beauty of the island itself.

Snorkelling, scuba diving, swimming, surfing and exploring the island's network of boardwalks and walkways are other popular pursuits.

Penguin Island has an interesting history. Seaforth McKenzie, an eccentric Canadian, lived on the island from about 1914 to 1926. He hollowed out several of the island's caves. Some were crudely furnished and had names like 'The Palace' and 'The Library'. Seaforth encouraged visitors and was crowned 'King of the Island' at a grandiose ceremony. It is now a conservation area and unsupervised visits to the island are restricted during the penguin breeding season, usually from June to about September. But for the rest of the year, visitors can enjoy the island's beaches and surrounds during daylight hours.

THE PENGUIN EXPERIENCE

Most little penguins land on Penguin Island an hour or two after sunset. They assemble just offshore in small groups or 'rafts' before landing, drawn together by their barking calls. The scientific name of the little penguin means 'little diver' and these birds are adept in the water. The little penguin is the smallest of the world's 17 penguin species. Adults stand about 40 centimetres tall and weigh about a kilogram, but birds in the Shoalwater area are larger than those elsewhere in Australia.

A specialised viewing centre (The Penguin Experience) has been established on the island for visitors to see the little penguins at close range during the day. The public can watch little penguins frolicking in the water and learn about how these little diving birds live and behave in the wild. The birds that live in this facility have either been rejected by their mothers as chicks, and raised by wildlife carers, or nursed back to health after injury. They would otherwise have died. They have now become so used to people that they would probably be unable to survive in the wild. Entry into the centre is included in the cost of the ferry ride or tour, which leaves from the mainland.

RESEARCH ON PENGUIN ISLAND

A research and management centre has been built on Penguin Island to manage the island and undertake important research. The centre, built with $120 000 sponsorship from WMC Resources Ltd, provides accommodation and facilities for researchers to study the area's wildlife and landforms. It is an important regional base for marine, island and coastal research.

SHOALWATER ISLANDS
MARINE PARK

The Penguin Experience

Jetty

PENGUIN ISLAND

0   100   200   300 m

Scale

FACING PAGE
Top: Inside The Penguin Experience.
Below: The WMC Resources Research and Management Centre.
Photos – Michael James/CALM

Little penguin. Photo – Babs & Bert Wells/CALM

FACING PAGE
Snorkelling at Penguin Island. Photo – Michael James/CALM

WHERE IS IT? 50 km south of Perth.

TRAVELLING TIME: Mersey Point at Rockingham, from which the ferry leaves, is less than 45 minutes drive from Perth.

ACCESS: The island is only open during the day. Ferry tours operate from Mersey Point from mid-September to early June and leave for Penguin Island on the hour throughout the day. You can take a cruise around the waters and islands of Shoalwater Bay, and view the sea lions lazing on Seal Island, with an opportunity to stroll around Penguin Island.

FACILITIES: The Penguin Experience, picnic tables, barbecues, toilets.

WHAT TO DO: Penguin viewing, swimming, picnicking, windsurfing, surfing, snorkelling.

WALKS:

Penguin Island Walktrail: You can purchase a pocket-sized colour booklet, *Discovering Penguin Island and the Shoalwater Islands Marine Park,* for just $5.95 from The Penguin Experience (proceeds from the book's sale go back into managing the island). A mud map and other information is included to help you discover and learn about the plants and animals of the island.

FURTHER ENQUIRIES: Penguin and Seal Island Cruises, phone (08) 9528 2004.

NEAREST CALM OFFICE: Rangers are stationed on the island and at Mersey Point in Rockingham. CALM's Marine and Coastal District Office is at 47 Henry Street, Fremantle, phone (08) 9432 5111.

Shoalwater Islands Marine Park

Picturesque submerged reefs and shipwrecks abound in the Rockingham area, less than an hours drive from Perth. Much of the underwater environment is protected in the Shoalwater Islands Marine Park. As well as encompassing an incredibly rich and diverse marine environment, the marine park surrounds a chain of unique limestone islands. These island nature reserves are significant in the ecology of a number of bird species. The park includes Shoalwater Bay, Warnbro Sound and the waters off Cape Peron.

Ferry tours operate from Mersey Point from mid-September to early June and feature a cruise around the waters and islands of Shoalwater Bay, with an opportunity to view the sea lions lazing on Seal Island, and to stroll around Penguin Island.

PLANTS AND ANIMALS

The islands of Shoalwater Bay abound with seabirds, many of which are seldom seen on the mainland. They are important seabird breeding sites. Sixteen species use the islands for courtship, nesting, feeding and roosting. Within the marine park there are breeding colonies of silver gulls, pied cormorants, fairy terns, bridled terns and Caspian terns. Crested terns are commonly seen, but don't usually breed on the islands.

The cavernous reefs surrounding the islands provide good snorkelling and diving. The reef areas support a variety of temperate and subtropical invertebrates, including sea stars, urchins and shellfish, as well as numerous fish species. Bottlenose dolphins are extremely common in the park's waters.

A colony of Australian sea lions haul out on Seal Island for most of the year and often fish and swim in nearby waters. The Australian sea lion is the rarest in the world and the species is given special protection under State legislation. Although they are one of our most attractive and interesting sea creatures, sea lions can deliver a nasty bite if aggravated. They are curious and may approach boats. To avoid disturbing the animals, which are territorial, you are asked not to land on the island.

Extensive areas of the sea floor are dominated by seagrass. These are important areas, since they provide nursery habitat for juvenile fish. The seagrass beds also help to stabilise the sandy floor.

WHERE IS IT? 50 km south of Perth.

TRAVELLING TIME: Less than 1 hour from central Perth.

TOTAL AREA: Approximately 6 545 ha.

ACCESS: Major public boat launching facilities are available at the Causeway, near Garden Island, and at two boat ramps on the foreshore of Safety Bay.

FACILITIES: The Penguin Experience, picnic facilities, toilets, drinking water, walkways and lookouts can be found on Penguin Island.

WHAT TO DO: Boating, fishing (outside sanctuary zones), swimming, windsurfing, boat tours, dive charters, sea kayaking tours. The western side of Penguin Island provides good surfing. Spearfishing is prohibited within certain zones and for divers using underwater breathing equipment. See the CALM publication *Dive & Snorkel Sites in Western Australia* for mud maps and further information on the dive sites below.

South Penguin Island: This shallow and very sheltered area is an ideal place to explore interesting underwater ledges and overhangs, lumps, low broken reef and seagrass areas. It is a good area for novice snorkellers, as it is only 2-5 m deep and fairly protected.

South end of Seal Island: This safe and enjoyable site is suitable for young snorkellers and family groups. Within a sheltered bay on the south side of Seal Island, it is protected in most weather conditions.

Cape Peron: A number of good snorkelling spots or shore dives can be found around Cape Peron, in 3-7 m of water.

The Sisters: This series of limestone reefs at the southern end of the Shoalwater Islands Marine Park offer snorkellers and scuba divers an excellent opportunity to experience an area rich in marine life.

First Rock: First Rock, the first large rock to the south of Penguin Island, is almost completely surrounded by reef, which is undercut by ledges and caves. Dive only in good weather conditions.

FURTHER ENQUIRIES: Penguin and Seal Island Cruises, phone (08) 9528 2004.

NEAREST CALM OFFICE: Rangers are stationed on Penguin Island and at Mersey Point, Rockingham. CALM's Marine and Coastal District Office is at 47 Henry Street, Fremantle, phone (08) 9432 5111.

FACING PAGE
Seven armed brittle star Photo – Peter & Margy Nicholas/Lochman Transparencies

Yalgorup National Park

Yalgorup National Park lies on the western edge of the Swan Coastal Plain, just south of the Dawesville Channel near Mandurah. The name Yalgorup is derived from two Nyoongar Aboriginal words; yalgor, meaning 'a swamp or lake', and up, a suffix meaning 'a place', an appropriate name as the park protects 10 lakes that run in a chain.

The park offers visitors panoramic views of beaches, dunes and lakes from several high spots. Peaceful settings among the patches of tuart forest and woodland, and sweeping views over the tranquil lakes, give the area a wilderness feel.

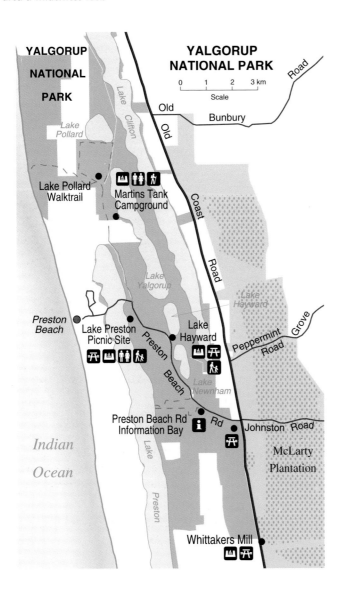

MICROSCOPIC MASTERBUILDERS

Some rather special formations on the edge of two lakes in the park provide a unique look at what life was like at the dawn of time.

Rock-like structures, known as thrombolites, on the edge of Lake Clifton are actually built by micro-organisms too small for the human eye to see. Like the famous stromatolites of Shark Bay, the structures of Lake Clifton contain living communities of diverse inhabitants with population densities of 3 000 million per square metre! Lake Clifton is one of only a few places in WA where living thrombolites survive. These peculiar structures live on the eastern edge of the lake and are most easily seen in March and April. Here, a boardwalk allows visitors to view these fascinating structures without damaging them.

The thrombolite-building micro-organisms of Lake Clifton resemble the earliest forms of life on Earth. These organisms are the only known form of life on Earth from 3 500 to 650 million years ago. The thrombolites and stromatolites they constructed dominated the clear, shallow seas and formed extensive reef tracts rivalling those of modern coral reefs. Similar organisms, for instance, helped to form the rich iron-ore deposits of the Hamersley Range, in the Pilbara, some 2 000 million years ago. At this time, oxygen made up only one per cent of the atmosphere. When there was no more iron to precipitate, the free oxygen leaked into the atmosphere until it formed 21 per cent of atmospheric gases.

Today, living examples of these once completely dominant organisms are restricted to only a few places. So why do thrombolites grow at Yalgorup? Scientists have suggested it is perhaps because Lake Clifton is associated with upwellings of fresh groundwater that is high in calcium carbonate. The micro-organisms living in this shallow lake environment are able to precipitate calcium carbonate from the waters as they photosynthesise, forming the mineralised structure which is the thrombolite.

WILDLIFE

The lakes provide important habitat for the international transequatorial waders that migrate from the northern hemisphere. These waders include the bar-tailed godwit, red-necked stint, greenshank, red knot, whimbrel and three species of sandpiper. Other waterbirds that use the lakes include the banded and black-winged stilts, red-necked avocet, hooded and red-capped plovers, Australian pelican and coot. The Yalgorup lakes support exceptionally high numbers of musk ducks, Pacific black ducks, black swans and shelducks.

The limestone ridges are covered with delicate heath species and include some special mallees, such as Fremantle mallee (*Eucalyptus foecunda*) and the rare limestone mallee (*E. petrensis*).

WHERE IS IT? 50 km south of Mandurah.

TOTAL AREA: 13 001 ha.

TRAVELLING TIME: 1 hour and 20 minutes from Perth, 45 minutes from Bunbury.

WHAT TO DO: Thrombolite viewing, picnicking, bushwalking, birdwatching, camping. Fishing and swimming at Preston Beach.

FACILITIES:

Lake Clifton (Mt John Road): Observation boardwalk over the thrombolites, information bay, toilets, tables.

Lake Hayward: Barbecues, picnic tables and toilets.

Martins Tank Lake: Campground, barbecues, tables, toilets and firewood.

WALKS:

Lake Pollard Trail: Moderate 2 hour, 6 km walk begins at the entrance to Martins Tank campground on Preston Beach Road (North) and traverses tuart and peppermint woodland rich in wildflowers to reach Lake Pollard, which is renowned for its high numbers of black swans between October and March.

Heathlands Walk: Moderate 4.5 km, 1½ hour walk. Begins at the information bay on Preston Beach Road and explores many different vegetation types, from towering tuarts to the delicate flowers of the limestone ridges.

NEAREST CALM OFFICE: CALM's Mandurah office is at Lot 31, Pinjarra Road, Mandurah, (08) 9582 9333.

Above: A boardwalk at Lake Clifton enables viewing of thrombolites. Photo – Jiri Lochman

Leschenault Peninsula Conservation Park

The Leschenault Peninsula is a finger-like projection that separates the Indian Ocean from the Leschenault Estuary. It is about 11 kilometres long and varies in width from 600 metres to 1 600 metres. Most of the Leschenault Peninsula Conservation Park is closed to motor vehicles, and you can only walk, boat or cycle in to this unique coastal area. It also provides the opportunity for a diverse range of ocean and estuary based water activities.

The coastal vegetation includes well developed stands of peppermint and tuart. There is also a small stand of the white mangrove, which, along with small stands in nearby Leschenault Inlet, are the most southerly occurrence of this plant in WA.

HISTORY

This scenic part of the coast has had a chequered history. Since European settlement, the Peninsula was mostly used for stock grazing. In 1838 Thomas Little purchased 741.4 hectares on Leschenault Peninsula on behalf of Charles Robert Prinsep, and named the homestead Belvidere in honour of the Prinsep mansion in Calcutta. Little managed the property to raise horses and cattle for the Indian Army.

John Boyle O'Reilly was one of 62 Irish political prisoners among 279 convicts who arrived at Fremantle in 1868. He was a member of the Fenian Movement, an organisation dedicated to achieving an independent Irish Republic. While working as a member of a convict road crew near Bunbury, O'Reilly escaped and made his way to the Leschenault Peninsula. He spent several weeks sheltering in the dense peppermint woodland on the peninsula, with the assistance of a local family, and eventually made his escape by boarding the *Gazelle*, an American whaler, on March 3, 1869. O'Reilly eventually settled in Boston, where he became a well-known humanitarian, writer, poet and orator. A monument erected to O'Reilly stands at the northern entry to Leschenault Peninsula.

From 1963 to 1990, Leschenault Peninsula was used as a disposal site for acid effluent produced as waste from the production of titanium dioxide. The effluent was pumped across the estuary in a pipeline and then into a series of ponds. Various Government agencies have spent more than $2.4 million to rehabilitate the former effluent disposal sites. In the late 1960s and throughout the 1970s, Belvidere became a commune for alternative lifestylers, with up to 14 houses, before the area was declared as a conservation park.

WATERBIRDS

The Leschenault Estuary is an important area for 62 different species of waterbird. They include various cormorants, the Australian pelican, straw-necked and sacred ibises, and the yellow-billed spoonbill. There are five species of heron: the great egret, little egret, white-faced heron, Pacific heron and rufous night-heron. The wetlands along the interface between the estuary and the peninsula, along with the shallow mudflats and seagrass meadows, contribute to the estuarine fish food supply, by providing insect larvae and plant material. In many instances, waterbirds of the open estuary breed in these fringing wetland areas. Seabirds recorded in the park include the little penguin and the Cape petrel.

WHERE IS IT? 150 km south of Perth, 22 km north of Bunbury and 30 km south-west of Harvey, via Buffalo Road, off the Old Coast Road.

TRAVELLING TIME: 30 minutes from Bunbury, 2 hours from Perth.

TOTAL AREA: 1 071 ha.

WHAT TO DO: Picnicking, bushwalking, camping, cycling, birdwatching, fishing.

FACILITIES: Barbecues, tables, toilets, lookout, dual use path for the shared use of walkers and cyclists. The Cut camping and picnic area and Tuart Grove picnic area are accessible by boat only. Firewood is provided at designated fireplaces only.

WALKS:

Belvidere Estuary Walk: Medium 4 km, 1½ hour loop. Head east from the Belvidere car park.

NEAREST CALM OFFICE: Central Forest Regional Office, North Boyanup Road, Bunbury, phone (08) 9725 4300.

View over the estuary. Photo – Jon Green/CALM

Top: Estuary foreshore. Photo – Gordon Roberts/CALM
Above: Black-winged stilt. Photo – Babs & Bert Wells/CALM
Left: Mangroves. Photo – Jon Green/CALM

Bunbury

First recorded by French explorer Captain de Freycinet aboard the *Geographe* in 1803, the townsite was originally named Port Leschenault. It was later renamed Bunbury after Lieutenant Bunbury, who suggested that a settlement be established here. Today, Bunbury is a bustling city that makes an ideal base from which to explore the beauty of the surrounding countryside. The city straddles long sandy beaches and the Leschenault Inlet.

Boulters Heights, a hill near the centre of Bunbury, has excellent views over the city, harbour, the coast and the Darling Range. Nearby is a waterfall and pedestrian walkway to the base of the hill.

Big Swamp, on Prince Philip Drive in South Bunbury, has an array of native bird life, including egrets, ducks and ibises. Bird hides and boardwalks have been built to facilitate birdwatching, and an excellent path circumnavigates the swamp. The adjacent Big Swamp Wildlife Park is also very popular with visitors and boasts a large walk-in aviary.

The results of an ancient volcanic lava flow, believed to have occurred 150 million years ago, can be seen on the beach at the northern end of Ocean Beach. The black Bunbury basalt rock can be seen here. The only other place in the South-West where this rock outcrops is at Black Point, in the D'Entrecasteaux National Park south-east of Augusta.

LESCHENAULT INLET

Mrs Evelyn Smith, known locally as the dolphin lady, began to feed the bottlenose dolphins in the Leschenault Inlet during the 1960s and continued until her death in the 1970s. A Dolphin Discovery Centre has since been established at Koombana Bay and the dolphins often visit the beach. You can learn more about these intelligent creatures by visiting the interpretive displays and theatre in the centre.

The inlet is also an ideal place to fish for the delectable blue manna crab. There are daily bag limits and minimum legal sizes, and all females carrying eggs must be thrown back into the water while they are still alive. Contact Fisheries WA for the latest rules and regulations. Follow a few common sense rules and blue manna crabs will be here to stay.

WHERE IS IT? 180 km south of Perth via the Old Coast Road.

TRAVELLING TIME: 2 hours from Perth.

WHAT TO DO: Picnicking, bushwalking, cycling, birdwatching, fishing.

FACILITIES: Full accommodation, shopping, dining and entertainment facilities. Sightseeing and other tours are available. The Dolphin Discovery Centre has a cafe and souvenir shop.

NEAREST CALM OFFICE: Central Forest Regional Office, North Boyanup Road, Bunbury, phone (08) 9725 4300.

FACING PAGE
Top right: Dolphins. Photo – Jiri Lochman
Below right: Basalt on Bunbury coast. Photo – Gordon Roberts

Bunbury Entertainment Centre. Photo – Dennis Sarson/Lochman Transparencies

Tuart Forest National Park

The narrow strip of tuart (*Eucalyptus gomphocephala*) forest that links Capel and Busselton is one of the special places of the South-West. The majestic tuart tree grows only on coastal limestone extending 200 kilometres on either side of Perth. The Tuart Forest National Park protects the largest remaining pure forest of tuart in the world. It also has the tallest and largest specimens of tuart trees on the Swan Coastal Plain. Some trees are more than 33 metres high and 10 metres in girth.

The Tuart Forest National Park is a day use area, with a number of beautiful scenic drives. In the open glades of the forest there are attractive picnic sites, roadside stops and scenic drives to enjoy.

HISTORY

Early records describe the tuart forest as being 'a beautiful open forest in which visibility was clear for a half mile in any direction' and stated that 'the natural grass was as high as a horse's wither'. Before European settlement, Aboriginal inhabitants took advantage of this abundance of grassland and the plentiful water to live well on the area's wildlife.

With the arrival of Europeans, coastal forest areas were cleared for settlement, timber and fuel. Because the tuart forest presented an open landscape, with a wide variety of grasses, its land was excellent for grazing cattle. The poisonous heartleaf (*Gastrolobium bilobum*) in the undergrowth was eradicated, and any native grasses unsuitable for grazing were soon replaced with exotic species.

The surface deposits of limestone also attracted early settlers. The lime kilns, at the northern end of the forest, were built in the mid-late 1800s and are now partially dilapidated. Park managers plan to conserve and restore the site of the lime kilns and eventually construct a car park, walktrail, viewing platform and interpretive facilities there.

Timber cutting operations were carried out throughout the 1800s. Wooden-railed, horse-drawn trams ran the length of the forest, hauling logs and timber products to the mills. Busselton's famous 1.8 kilometre long jetty was built to service the timber industry, and sleepers and other timber cutting relics can still be seen in the park.

In the early 1900s, local property owners and the timber industry lobbied the government to purchase the remaining tracts of forest back from the estates of Governor Stirling, to secure its use for future timber production and railway purposes. This culminated in 1919 with the passing of the Forests Act and the gazettal of the areas as State Forests 1 and 2 – the first publicly-owned forests in the State.

In 1920 a sawmill was erected across the estuary at Wonnerup Beach, some 10 kilometres east of Busselton. A small jetty was built off the beach and shallow draft boats took the timber to schooners anchored in Geographe Bay. The mill operated for about 10 years. After the Second World War, wood was again in strong demand. A new mill was built at Ludlow in 1955 and it worked on and off until 1974. The national park was declared in 1987.

WILDFLOWERS AND WILDLIFE

The park's vegetation also includes a number of isolated and remnant populations of several plant species, normally associated with WA's South Coast. There is also a thriving community of fungi, including some species yet to be named. Last, but certainly not least, the Tuart Forest National Park provides an abundance of nesting hollows, used by many species of waterbird that feed in the adjacent wetlands.

The park also protects WA's largest remaining wild population of the threatened western ringtail possum. This is largely because old tuart trees contain many hollows, while the dense secondary storey of peppermint trees supplies their major source of food. The forest is also home to the densest population of brushtail possums ever recorded in the State. Other residents include the brush-tailed phascogale, bush rat, kangaroo, quenda (also known as the southern brown bandicoot) and at least 11 species of birds of prey and nocturnal birds.

Nearby Wonnerup House, built in 1859 and beautifully restored, is managed by the National Trust. It provides a glimpse into the lives of the pioneers and is open daily from 12-4 pm.

Left: Historic Wonnerup House. Photo – Marie Lochman

WHERE IS IT? 15 km north-east of Busselton.

TRAVELLING TIME: 10-15 minutes from Busselton.

TOTAL AREA: 2 049 ha.

WHAT TO DO: Picnicking, scenic driving, bushwalking, night spotlighting for forest animals.

FACILITIES:

Layman Picnic Site - Bird hide, picnic tables, barbecues, toilets and information panels, walktrails (see below).

Ludlow - Tuart House Forest Education Centre, Tuart Visitor Centre, native garden display, walktrails (see below), toilets, picnic tables.

WALKS:

Sawpit Walk: Easy 1 km, 30 minute loop walk. Beginning at the Layman picnic site, it takes in the historic sites of the area including an old sawpit.

Possum Night Spotlighting Trail: Easy 1.5 km, 1 hour walk. Also beginning at Layman picnic site, this self-guided trail is designed to be completed at night with a spotlight or large torch. You are likely to see the threatened western ringtail possum and the more common brushtail possum. Red reflectors and information plaques guide the way.

NEAREST CALM OFFICE: South West Capes District Office, 14 Queen Street, Busselton, phone (08) 9752 1677.

Right: Tuart trees. Photo – Jay Sarson/Lochman Transparencies
Below: Ringtail possum. Photo – Babs & Bert Wells/CALM

Busselton

Overlooking the calm waters of Geographe Bay, Busselton is known for its broad sandy beaches and pleasant holiday atmosphere. Named after a French sailor, the Vasse River makes a delightful grassy picnic area adjacent to the Rotary Childrens' Playground. The town is a magnificent launching point to explore the parks, marine environment and other natural attractions of the South-West Capes region.

BUSSELTON JETTY

One of the town's major attractions is the Busselton Jetty, the second longest wooden jetty in the southern hemisphere. Train rides run the length of the jetty every day, and there is a shady picnic and barbecue area on the nearby beachfront. The first jetty (158.4 metres long) was built in 1865, from giant karri hardwoods. It was used by whalers and other vessels. Further extensions were made in 1875, 1884, 1887, 1890, 1894, 1895 and 1896 as silt built up around the structure. It is now 1 799 metres long.

The jetty is a magnet for anglers and scuba divers. Although many invertebrates inhabit the pylons close to the shore, the displays of coral and sponge are most spectacular at the end of the jetty. It is also an excellent night dive, because it is almost impossible to get lost. Thousands of invertebrates have built up around the pylons, creating a bevy of colours and forms. Many of these animals are normally only found in deeper waters or under reef ledges, but are able to exist here because the jetty protects them from the direct rays of the sun.

VASSE-WONNERUP WETLANDS

The Vasse-Wonnerup wetlands, surrounding Busselton, are among the State's most important. They support a large number of waterbirds and waders. Local species gather in large numbers in late summer and early autumn, as wetlands and dams dry up in inland agricultural areas. More than 30 000 birds and 77 species at one time have been recorded on the water bodies.

Vasse-Wonnerup has the highest number of black-winged stilts in Australia. It is one of the five most important sites in Australia for the red-necked avocet. The wetlands support the highest number of breeding black swans known in Western Australia, with about 200 pairs. They contain more pelicans, great egrets and yellow-billed spoonbills than any other south-western wetland. Vasse-Wonnerup has the third highest number of bird species recorded at any south-western wetland.

WHERE IS IT? 229 km south of Perth, 59 km from Nannup.

TRAVELLING TIME: 2½ hours drive from Perth, 40 minutes from Bunbury.

WHAT TO DO: Picnicking, scenic driving, fishing, scuba diving, swimming, whale watching, cycling, abseiling.

FACILITIES: Full accommodation, shopping, dining and entertainment facilities. Sightseeing tours, dive and fishing charters and four-wheel-drive safaris are available.

NEAREST CALM OFFICE: South West Capes District Office, 14 Queen Street, Busselton, phone (08) 9752 1677.

Above left: Vasse-Wonnerup wetlands. Photo – Geoff Taylor/Lochman Transparencies
Left: Busselton's 1 799 metre jetty. Photo – John Kleczkowski/Lochman Transparencies

FACING PAGE
The jetty is a magnet for scuba divers. Photo – Peter & Margy Nicholas/Lochman Transparencies

Dunsborough

Dunsborough is a popular coastal playground set around a shallow bay. A range of amenities and attractions are provided in or surround the seaside town. They include galleries, wineries and wildlife parks.

Meelup, Eagle Bay and Bunker Bay lie north-west from Dunsborough and are largely protected from ocean swells by Cape Naturaliste. These beautiful, sheltered bays provide magnificent family swimming areas. It is also worth donning snorkel and fins to explore the marine life. The diversity of colourful fish is surprising. Cuttlefish and western blue devils lurk under ledges, while a blaze of sponges, soft corals and other marine life coats the submerged rocks.

Further offshore, the 2 750 tonne, 140 metre long *HMAS Swan* lies in 30 metres of clear water and has become a magnet for scuba divers. The navigation and antennae tower is about eight metres below the surface, with the upper deck at about 15 metres. The Geographe Bay Artificial Reef Society cleaned *HMAS Swan* thoroughly before it was sunk to prevent oil, silt or debris hampering divers, and more than 10 000 spectators lined the shores or watched from boats when she was scuttled in December 1997. A permit is required for privately owned and commercial boats to take divers to the scuttled ship. The best way to see *HMAS Swan* is by means of a dive charter. Local dive shops offer charters to see the outside of the ship, while an Advanced Wreck Dive Course can be completed to enable more experienced divers to explore inside the ship.

WHERE IS IT? 255 km south of Perth.

TRAVELLING TIME: 3 hours from Perth, 1 hour from Bunbury.

WHAT TO DO: Picnicking, scenic driving, fishing, scuba diving, swimming, whale watching, caving, surfing, camping, beachcombing.

FACILITIES: Accommodation, shopping, dining and entertainment facilities. Sightseeing tours, dive and fishing charters, and four-wheel-drive safaris are available.

WALKS:

Eagle Bay to Rocky Point: Easy 2 km, 40 minute walk through peppermint, heathland and melaleuca communities and along the beach, from the most northerly car park at Eagle Bay to Rocky Point.

Bunker Bay: Easy 2.5 km, 1 hour walk through heath, with breathtaking views of the coast and lookouts, from which you may see whales.

NEAREST CALM OFFICE: South West Capes District Office, 14 Queen Street, Busselton, phone (08) 9752 1677.

Bunker Bay. Photo – Chris Garnett/CALM

Yallingup

Yallingup is known for its magnificent caves, breathtaking scenery and crashing surf. Yallingup Beach is one of the State's top surfing beaches. Smiths Beach is popular with surfers and boogie boarders and has excellent fishing. Wineries, galleries and other attractions also draw visitors, while a network of walktrails meanders around the town.

CANAL ROCKS

At Canal Rocks, in the Leeuwin-Naturaliste National Park, the granitic rocks which jut out into the ocean are separated by a series of canals that have been hollowed out by the sea. You can traverse the canals by a series of narrow bridges and clamber over the rocks to marvel at the ocean's relentless power.

It is thought that around 600 million years ago, the original rocks here were subjected to a period of intense heat and pressure, causing changes in their structure and mineral composition. They became layered and folded, forming bands of varying hardness which tend to lie parallel to the present coastline. Bands of weaker rock have been eroded more easily by the sea, creating the spectacular 'canal' formation.

NGILGI CAVE

Ngilgi Cave was discovered by Europeans in 1899. According to Aboriginal legend, a bad spirit known as Wolgine lived in the cave, which used to run down to the sea. The tribespeople were terrified of him; they thought that he was responsible for the scarcity of food and water, and believed that anyone entering the cave would suffer a horrible death at his hands. So they enlisted the help of a good spirit, Ngilgi, who caused a great storm which drove Wolgine into the main cavern of the cave, where Ngilgi forced him through the roof and he was banished forever.

Ngilgi Cave is renowned for its spectacular shawls and is open daily. Tours are semi-guided and leave every half hour. Fully guided Adventure Caving (for adventurers over 15 years of age and in good health) or Torchlight Tours (suitable for all ages) are also available.

WHERE IS IT? 263 km south of Perth.

TRAVELLING TIME: 3 hours from Perth, 1 hour from Bunbury.

WHAT TO DO: Picnicking, scenic driving, fishing, scuba diving, swimming, whale watching, cave tours, surfing, camping.

FACILITIES: Full accommodation, shopping, dining and entertainment facilities. Sightseeing tours, dive and fishing charters and four-wheel-drive safaris are available.

WALKS:

Wardanup Trail: Moderate 5 km, 2½ hour loop.

Torpedo Trail: Easy 2 km, 1 hour loop follows the coast from Yallingup to Torpedo Rocks, then turns inland to return to town.

Ghost Trail: Easy 700 m, 30 minute track between Caves House and the sea.

Caves Trail: Easy 500 m, 15 minute path between Caves House and Ngilgi Cave.

Quenda Trail: This moderate 4 km, 2 hour trail is named after the bandicoot which may be seen in the area around dusk.

NEAREST CALM OFFICE: South West Capes District Office, 14 Queen Street, Busselton, phone (08) 9752 1677.

Ngilgi Cave. Photo – Dennis Sarson/Lochman Transparencies

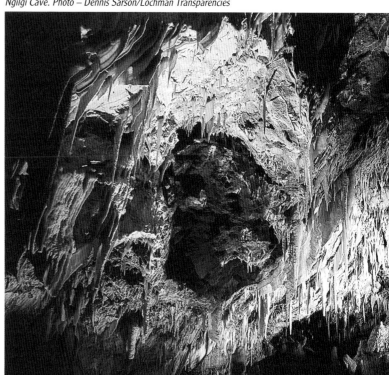

Leeuwin-Naturaliste National Park

Leeuwin-Naturaliste National Park stretches for 120 km, from Bunker Bay in the north to Augusta in the south. Rugged sea cliffs, windswept granite headlands, and formations such as Canal Rocks and Sugarloaf Rock dominate the coastline, interspersed with curving beaches, sheltered bays and long, rocky shorelines. On the northern shores of Cape Naturaliste, a series of quiet bays lead to the Cape. Protected from the prevailing south-westerly winds, these areas are popular for swimming, fishing or beachcombing.

COASTAL PURSUITS

Between May and June, huge schools of salmon head north up the coast on their annual spawning run. The salmon, between four and eight kilograms, are keenly sought by anglers with both lures and bait. Bag limits apply. Full details are available from the Fisheries Department.

Surfing is also popular at many well-known breaks on the western coast, such as Smiths Beach and Yallingup. Coastal walktrails and steps down sand dunes have been provided at many places to help prevent erosion.

Most roads in the area are sealed. Gravel roads are usually suitable for two-wheel-drive vehicles. There are three campgrounds within the park, at Conto, Point Road and Boranup. Fees apply and will be collected by a ranger on site. There are only basic facilities such as barbecues, firewood, toilets and tables. At Conto Campground there is also water. There are no powered sites or showers.

WHERE IS IT? 70 km south of Bunbury.

TRAVELLING TIME: 1½ hours from Bunbury.

WHAT TO DO: Picnicking, scenic driving, fishing, scuba diving, swimming, whale watching, caving, surfing, camping.

FACILITIES: Accommodation, shopping, dining and entertainment facilities are available in the towns of Dunsborough, Yallingup, Margaret River and Augusta. Sightseeing tours, dive and fishing charters, and four-wheel-drive safaris are also available.

WALKS:

Cape Naturaliste Track: Medium 3.2 km, 1 to 1½ hour walk with views over Cape Naturaliste. Travels through small limestone 'pinnacles' en route to a stunning whale lookout.

Cape to Cape Walk Track: This 140 km track from Cape Naturaliste to Cape Leeuwin can be broken into a number of shorter sections.

Canal Rocks to Wyadup: Medium 4 km, 2 hour return walk with outstanding views. Begin at the car park above and overlooking Canal Rocks. Look for the Cape to Cape walktrail markers.

NEAREST CALM OFFICE: South West Capes District Office, 14 Queen Street, Busselton, phone (08) 9752 1677.

Coast near Canal Rocks. Photo – Jiri Lochman

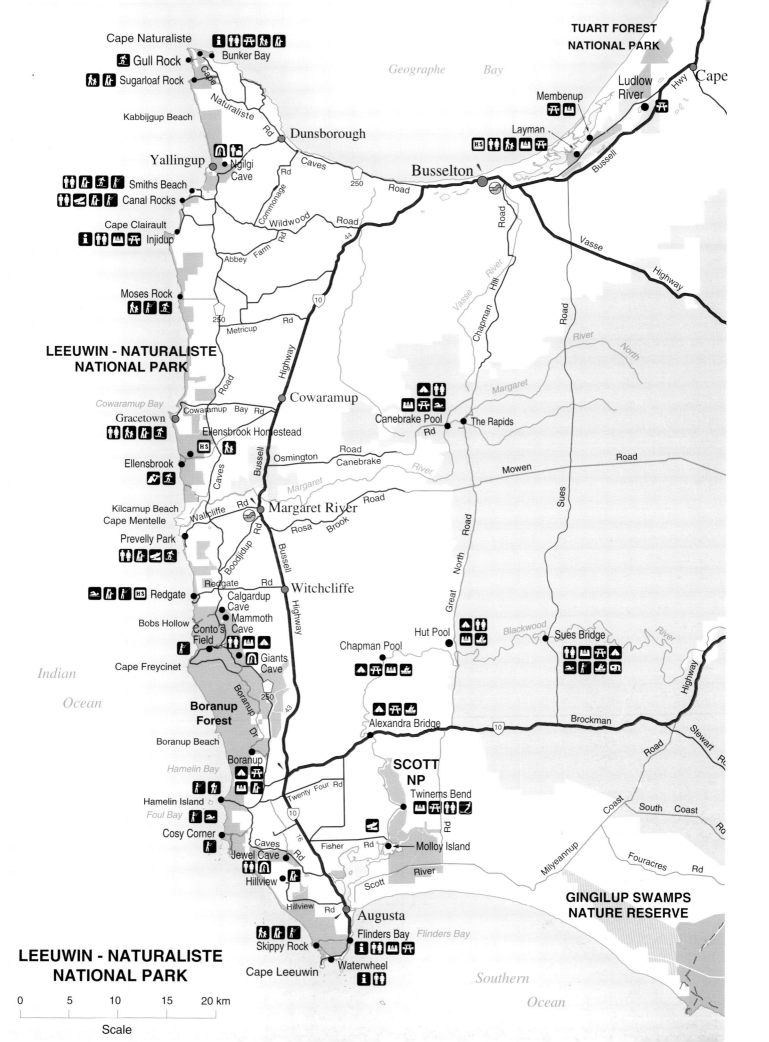

Cape Naturaliste
Gull Rock
Sugarloaf Rock
Bunker Bay
Kabbijgup Beach

TUART FOREST
NATIONAL PARK

Geographe   Bay

Ludlow
River   Cape

Membenup

Layman

Dunsborough
Caves

Busselton

Yallingup
Ngilgi
Cave

Smiths Beach
Canal Rocks

Cape Clairault
Injidup

Commonage Rd
Wildwood Road
Abbey Farm Rd
Metricup Rd

Vasse   River
Chapman Hill
Road

Vasse

Road

Highway

LEEUWIN - NATURALISTE
NATIONAL PARK

Moses Rock

Cowaramup Bay
Gracetown

Ellensbrook Homestead
Ellensbrook

Cowaramup

Cowaramup Bay Rd
Osmington
Road
Canebrake

Margaret   River

Canebrake Pool   The Rapids
Rd

Mowen   Road

Margaret   River

Sues   Road

Kilcarnup Beach
Cape Mentelle
Prevelly Park

Margaret River

Wallcliffe   Rd
Rosa   Brook   Road

Boodjidup Rd
Bussell

Great North Road

Redgate
Bobs Hollow
Conto's
Field
Cape Freycinet

Calgardup
Cave
Mammoth
Cave
Giants
Cave

Redgate   Rd
Witchcliffe

Highway

Chapman Pool

Hut Pool

Blackwood

Sues Bridge

River

Boranup
Forest
Boranup Beach
Hamelin Bay
Boranup

Boranup Dr

43
250

Alexandra Bridge

SCOTT
NP

Brockman

Stewart Rd

Road

Coast

South   Coast

Hamelin Island
Foul Bay
Cosy Corner

Twenty Four Rd

10

Twinems Bend

Molloy Island

Fisher   Rd

Milyeannup   Coast

Fouracres   Rd

Jewel Cave
Hillview

Hillview

Caves Rd

16

Scott   River

Augusta

GINGILUP SWAMPS
NATURE RESERVE

Skippy Rock
Cape Leeuwin

LEEUWIN - NATURALISTE
NATIONAL PARK

Flinders Bay   Flinders Bay

Waterwheel

Indian

Ocean

Southern

Ocean

0   5   10   15   20 km

Scale

Margaret River

At Margaret River, lush green farmland intermixes with tall karri and spectacular coastline. Timber cutting and the dairy industry were once the mainstays of the local economy. Today tourism and wine-making are becoming increasingly important. There are white sandy beaches interspersed with dramatic coastal cliffs. There is sparkling water and crashing surf. Dozens of vineyards, restaurants, cafes and galleries are packed with art, much of it produced by the alternative lifestylers that have flocked to the area in droves. The local architecture features homes constructed from mud brick and natural timbers, with corrugated iron roofs.

A favourite pastime is scenic driving. Visitors often meander along Caves Road, stopping to enjoy its many natural attractions while sampling the local produce. Though it is a relatively new industry here, this fertile region produces some of the best wines in the world. The region's dairy heritage means it is also a great place to enjoy the locally produced 'boutique' cheeses and yoghurts.

MARGARET RIVER COAST

Between Cowaramup Bay and Karridale is some of the most rugged and inaccessible coastline within the Leeuwin-Naturaliste National Park. Facing due west, the coastal cliffs and rocky shoreline bear the brunt of giant ocean swells generated across thousands of miles of ocean by the prevailing westerly and south-westerly winds. Punctuated along the coast are scenic lookouts from which to marvel at the ocean's beauty and power.

One of the loveliest spots to visit is the historic homestead at Ellensbrook, which is managed by the National Trust. The turn-off to Ellensbrook Homestead, off Caves Road, is nine kilometres from Margaret River. Alfred Bussell arrived in Western Australia in 1830, and later pioneered the Margaret River area. In 1857 he built Ellensbrook as a home for his wife, Ellen, out of crushed shell and limestone. They lived here until 1865, when they moved to Wallcliffe House at the mouth of the Margaret River. A walktrail constructed by CALM leads to a cave and the delightful Meekadarabee Falls, which is at its best in winter and spring.

Just 10 kilometres west of the town, the Margaret River widens in a graceful sweep and meets the Indian Ocean. Calgardup Beach, Redgate, is the location where Grace Bussell and Sam Isaacs rode out on horseback to rescue survivors of the *Georgette* in 1876.

In the right weather conditions there are some enjoyable and safe places to snorkel, such as at Prevelly and Gnarabup. Scattered along this coast are sheltered bays suitable for launching small boats, such as Kilcarnup, Cowaramup Bay and Prevelly. Tracks to the more isolated surfing and fishing spots on the coast are often suitable only for four-wheel-drive, because of the rough limestone that protrudes from the road surfaces.

CAVES OF THE CAPE

The limestone that forms the rugged coastline is also riddled with caves. Two self-guided unlit caves, Calgardup and Giants, were tourist caves around the turn of the century. People should wear old clothing and sturdy footwear and ring the Calgardup Information Centre to check opening times, as they vary seasonally. Torches and hard hats are supplied.

Calgardup Cave is spectacular because of the water covering the floor of three caverns. The special effects from the reflections of the water surface are something to see. Elevated platforms have been built through the cave so people can enjoy the exquisite beauty at their own pace and without a guide. You will not get lost. Educational signs are placed throughout the cave. Adventure sections of Calgardup Cave are available with a guide and can be arranged by talking to staff at the entrance.

Giants Cave has huge caverns and is about 800 metres long. The cave is unique in that it is a through cave, meaning you can enter a spectacular doline and reappear out of another. Elevated platforms and marked paths are provided, so getting lost is not an issue. There are numerous spots where the caver will want to stop, relax and absorb the world-class cave formations.

There are other caves you can visit on the ridge. For adventure tours, there are caves which need a trip leader. Contact the Calgardup Information Centre on (08) 9757 7422. For guided tours into lit caves contact the two local tourist associations for tour times. The Cape Naturaliste Tourism Association runs Ngilgi Cave, phone (08) 9755 2152, while Augusta-Margaret River Tourist Association conducts regular tours of Mammoth, Lake and Jewel Caves, phone (08) 9758 4541.

Mammoth Cave, about 21 kilometres south of Margaret River, is extremely large and has many long chambers and smaller passages. During winter, a stream flows through it, creating reflections and giving the cave new life. The cave features stalactites, stalagmites and large columns where the two formations meet. A coloured shawl is prominent in one of the smaller chambers.

The WA Museum has found several fossils left there by Aboriginal people who used the entrance cavern for shelter. The jawbone of an extinct marsupial about the size of a cow is visible in the wall of this cavern. Entry to the cave is from the eastern side, and the exit is on the western side of Caves Road. A short bushwalk through the forest takes visitors back to their cars.

Lake Cave, located three kilometres south of Mammoth Cave, is one of the deepest tourist caves. A series of stairways and paths descend through a large 'crater' with huge karri trees growing from its depths. The lake never dries up and the path runs along its edge. It is heavily decorated

with fragile white calcite straws, shawls, stalactites and stalagmites. A prominent feature is the Suspended Table, a large flat area of flowstone supported just above the lake from above by two large columns.

Cave Works, near Lake Cave on Cave Road, is a discovery centre where visitors can walk through a cave model featuring a flowing stream. Interactive touch screens allow visitors to explore subjects such as cave mineralogy, bones of our distant past and historical information. Universally accessible boardwalks lead to a viewing platform, where visitors can glimpse into the depths of Lake Cave. There is also a theatrette and tearoom.

Cape to Cape walktrail near Conto Beach. Photo – Chris Garnett/CALM

WHERE IS IT? 277 km south of Perth.

TRAVELLING TIME: 3½ hours from Perth.

WHAT TO DO: Picnicking, scenic driving, fishing, scuba diving, swimming, whale watching, cave tours, surfing, camping, cycling.

Rails to Trails Cycle Trail: Follows an old railway line from Margaret River to near Cowaramup.

FACILITIES: Full accommodation, shopping, dining and entertainment facilities. Sightseeing tours, dive charters and four-wheel-drive safaris are available. Leeuwin-Naturaliste National Park has campgrounds with basic facilities. Fees apply and no bookings are available.

Conto Campground - A basic camping experience within the national park. Turn down Conto Road from Caves Road. Facilities include toilets, barbecues, tables, water, individual sites in the bush.

Point Road Campground - Head down Conto Road to the coast and drive away from the coast along Point Road. Facilities include toilets, barbecues, tables and individual sites.

WALKS:

Meekadarabee Falls: Easy 2 km, 40 minute walk from the historic Ellensbrook Homestead to the delightful Meekadarabee Falls. The trail and all facilities are accessible to the disabled.

Ten Mile Brook Dam Walk: Hard 14 km return trail through karri forest from 'Old Kate' in Rotary Park to the Ten Mile Brook Dam.

Pine Plantation Walk: Easy 1.7 km walk through giant pines from Carters Road Trailhead.

Big Brook Trail: Easy 3.4 km walk along a brook taking in numerous old railway bridges.

Old Chimney Walk: Easy 2.7 km walk to an old curved brick chimney.

Margaret River Heritage Trail: A network of three trails along the Margaret River commencing at Rotary Park.

Cape to Cape Walk Track: Pick up this 140 km track at many points along the coast between Cape Naturaliste and Cape Leeuwin.

NEAREST CALM OFFICE: Two rangers, one based at Caves Road, Cowaramup, and one at Bussell Highway, Margaret River, patrol this part of the Leeuwin-Naturaliste National Park. CALM's Margaret River Office is at Bussell Highway, Margaret River, phone (09) 9757 2422. Information can also be obtained from the Calgardup Information Centre on (08) 9737 7422.

Ellensbrook. Photo – Lochman Transparencies/CALM

FACING PAGE
Meekadarabee Falls. Photo – Marie Lochman

Boranup Forest

Boranup Forest, within the Leeuwin-Naturaliste National Park, lies between Caves Road and the coast, and creates a powerful contrast with the rest of the coastline. Tall pale-barked karri trees, reaching heights of 60 metres or more, dominate the hilly slopes and valleys. Gravel roads suitable for two-wheel-drive vehicles wind through the forest to picnic and camping spots. A short walk takes you to Boranup Lookout, which gives sweeping views over the forest and the coast west to Hamelin Bay.

Boranup is an Aboriginal word that means 'place of the male dingo'. Sadly, however, these wild Australian dogs have now been exterminated from the Boranup area and from most of the South-West, after gaining a reputation as sheep killers.

Boranup is an extraordinary place for several reasons other than its sheer beauty. This is the furthest west that karri, the third tallest tree in the world, grows. The Boranup Forest is isolated from the main body of the karri belt, more than 100 kilometres to the east, by the grey infertile sands and lower rainfall of the Donnybrook Sunklands. Elsewhere in the South-West, karri grows almost exclusively on deep red clay loams. At Boranup it grows in limestone-based soils.

Waterbush and karri hazel form a dense understorey beneath the giant trees, and in spring white clematis, purple hovea and coral creepers add vivid colours to the cool green of the forest.

FACING PAGE
Boranup Forest. Photo – Cliff Winfield

Cosy Corner. Photo – Marie Lochman

HISTORY

The Boranup Forest is about 100 years old. It is a regrowth forest. The Government granted Maurice Coleman Davies a 42 year lease at Boranup in 1882. Two thirds of the land was forested with jarrah and marri, and the rest with karri. The Hamelin jetty was built promptly, 600 metres long and capable of berthing three ships at a time with steam cranes alongside. Fresh water was laid on from a spring and telephone facilities were established to the company's head office. The Karridale Mill, the most advanced in the colony, began operations in 1884. In 1891, a new steam mill was commissioned at Boranup, but was destroyed by fire a few years later and promptly replaced with a bigger one at Jarrahdene in 1895.

Davies treated his workers as though they were a big family. Although wages were low – between seven and 13 shillings per day – the company provided workers with a cottage, rent free. It paid for a doctor and a clergyman and built a hospital, town hall, school, racecourse and a well-stocked library. Consumables, including fresh fruit and vegetables from the company orchards and gardens and meat from its farm, as well as every conceivable item, could be bought from the company's store. The company had an agreement with the workers allowing a 10 per cent mark-up on Perth prices to cover freight.

The last mill at Karridale closed in 1913. The timber yard at Hamelin Bay is now an attractive camping area, shaded by coastal peppermints. In 1961, fierce wildfires seared through the Boranup Forest, and destroyed the last traces of Karridale, which once housed more than 800 people.

WHERE IS IT? 20 km from Margaret River and 20 km from Augusta.

TRAVELLING TIME: 30 minutes from Margaret River or Augusta.

WHAT TO DO: Picnicking, scenic driving, camping, bushwalking.

FACILITIES: Tables, barbecues, toilets. There is a campground with basic facilities. Fees apply and no bookings are available.

Boranup Campground - Off the southern end of Boranup Drive. Facilities include barbecues, toilets and individual sites.

WALKS:

Boranup Lookout: Easy 600 m track to a lookout over Hamelin Bay and inland, to farmland and forests.

Cape to Cape Walk Track: A 140 km track from Cape Naturaliste to Cape Leeuwin.

NEAREST CALM OFFICE: Margaret River Office, Bussell Highway, Margaret River, phone (09) 9757 2322.

Augusta

The coastline that runs south of the Boranup Forest to Augusta offers sweeping coastal scenery, isolated fishing spots, sheer cliffs plunging into deep water, sheltered bays for swimming and curved beaches for combing. The majority of it is protected in the Leeuwin-Naturaliste National Park.

Hamelin Bay, once the shipping depot for the Karridale timber industry, is in the heart of the Leeuwin-Naturaliste National Park. Here, a fully serviced caravan and camping area, shaded by spreading peppermints, is located less than 500 metres from the beach, and looks out over the tiny islands, reefs and clear waters of Hamelin Bay. Other caravan parks are available in nearby towns.

The town of Augusta is perfectly situated at the junction of the Blackwood River and Flinders Bay. It is Western Australia's third oldest settlement. Visitors can enjoy safe beaches and a wide choice of fishing grounds in the river and estuary, or from beaches or rocks (if care is taken).

LIMESTONE CAVES

Jewel Cave is eight kilometres north of Augusta. Entry is through a huge, spectacular cavern. The cave contains the longest straw of any tourist cave in the world, at just over 5.9 metres. There is also a huge area of flowstone, which looks like karri forest, and a stalagmite estimated to weigh 20 tonnes. The cave was named after a smaller section known as the Jewel Casket and its crystal formations. Guided tours of about one hour are available.

The Moondyne Adventure Cave was recently developed. It gives visitors the opportunity to explore the hidden cave wilderness, while being guided by experienced tour guides during the course of a two hour tour. Both caves are open every day except Christmas. Tickets are available from the guides at each cave entrance prior to each tour. Detailed information on tour times are available from the Augusta-Margaret River Tourist Association, phone (08) 9758 4541.

LIGHTHOUSE AND WATERWHEEL

Cape Leeuwin was named by Flinders in 1801 after the Dutch exploration ship the *Leeuwin* (which means 'lioness'), which visited the area in 1622. The old lighthouse, which is still in use, is open daily for tours and gives views west and east over the meeting place of two great oceans: the Indian Ocean and the Southern Ocean. Sixteen ships were wrecked around Cape Leeuwin before the lighthouse was officially opened there by WA Premier John Forrest in 1896. Built by timber tycoon Maurice Coleman Davies, with the clockwork apparatus and kerosene lantern designed by C Y O'Connor, the 56 metre tall lighthouse operated in original condition until 1982, when it was converted to hydraulics and electricity.

The nearby waterwheel is also worth a visit. It was built to power a hydraulic ram, which would pump water from the nearby swamp to supply the lighthouse and keepers' cottages.

WHALES AND OTHER WONDERS

On July 30 1986, Flinders Bay to the east of Cape Leeuwin was the site of one of the world's most successful whale rescues. Townspeople, visitors, wildlife officers, surfers, forestry workers and a host of other volunteers from every walk of life laboured for two days and nights in the freezing surf off Augusta's town beach to relaunch a school of 114 stranded false killer whales. The whales, between two and five metres long, started to come ashore at 7.15 am on Wednesday morning. By Friday, 96 of the whales were successfully herded out of the bay by boardriders and boats. A memorial to the rescue has been established overlooking the town beach.

In the winter to spring months, whale watching is very popular in Flinders Bay. Both humpback and southern right whales frequent the area. During whale watching excursions, people are also taken out to view the colony of New Zealand fur seals on the rocky islands. The fur seals only reappeared in Augusta during the last 20 years, after having been decimated by sealers last century.

There are many wonderful diving spots in Flinders Bay, Hamelin Bay and Cosy Corner. The many reefs are riddled with caves and overhangs. The caves are home to fish such as scalyfin, western blue devils, red-lipped morwong and western foxfish. They are mostly curious and seem to have little fear of people. Cuttlefish, eagle rays and harlequin fish can also be seen lurking under ledges. You can occasionally encounter a giant blue groper, which is now uncommon on WA's western coast due to fishing pressure. These magnificent fish grow up to 1.6 metres long.

FACING PAGE
Top right: Picnic area at Barrack Point.
Right: Lighthouse and waterwheel. Photos – Bill Belson/Lochman Transparencies

WHERE IS IT? 320 km south of Perth.

TRAVELLING TIME: 4 hours from Perth.

WHAT TO DO: Picnicking, scenic driving, scenic flights, fishing, scuba diving, swimming, whale watching, cave touring, surfing, camping, Blackwood River tours, lighthouse tours.

FACILITIES: Full accommodation, shopping and dining facilities. Sightseeing tours, dive charters and whale watching tours are available.

WALKS:

Cape to Cape Walk Track: This 140 km track from Cape Naturaliste to Cape Leeuwin can be broken into shorter sections.

- **Cosy Corner to Skippy Rock:** Challenging 20 km full day hike for experienced walkers. The terrain is magnificent but rugged, and involves long stretches of sand and scrambles along narrow rock platforms. Vehicle pick-up essential.

- **Hamelin Bay to Cosy Corner:** Medium 13 km, 4 hour walk with magnificent views from the Hamelin Bay boat ramp to Cosy Corner and back. It involves some easy scrambling and negotiating short, steep sections.

- **Waterwheel to Skippy Rock:** Medium 3 km, 1 hour walk via beach, rocks and bush begins at the Leeuwin Waterwheel, near the Cape Leeuwin Lighthouse in Augusta.

NEAREST CALM OFFICE: Margaret River Office, Bussell Highway, Margaret River (09) 9757 2322.

Scott National Park

Originally selected for stock grazing by early settlers in the 1870s, Scott National Park features peaceful river scenes and pristine bushland, inhabited by many different animals and birds of the South-West. Straddling the eastern bank of the Blackwood Estuary and the lower reaches of the Blackwood River, the park protects open jarrah and marri woodlands, swamps and riverside vegetation. Large expanses of low heathland, interspersed with mounds supporting stands of taller vegetation, cover the Scott River plain.

The park's heath is studded with holly-leaf banksia (*Banksia ilicifolia*), Scott River banksia (*Banksia meisneri*), Meisner's woollybush (*Adenanthos meisneri*) and the basket flower (*Adenanthos obovatus*). This heath is excellent habitat for honey possums. This tiny nocturnal marsupial is highly specialised for feeding on nectar and pollen. Its long, pointed snout and brush-tipped tongue are perfectly suited for probing the flowers of banksias and other plants. Apart from some bats, the honey possum is the only mammal in the world that feeds exclusively on nectar and pollen.

Only one area in the park has facilities. Twinems Bend, accessible only by boat, is a popular waterski area. Toilets, tables and barbecues are provided here. Fires are permitted only in the fireplaces.

WHERE IS IT? 60 km east of Augusta by road.

TRAVELLING TIME: 1½ hours from Margaret River or Augusta.

TOTAL AREA: 3 273 ha.

WHAT TO DO: Fishing, swimming, boating, picnicking and bushwalking. However, large areas are covered by water during winter and are impassable, and dieback is easily spread by vehicles at this time. Twinems Bend, accessible only by boat, is a popular waterski area.

FACILITIES: Barbecues, toilets, picnic tables.

NEAREST CALM OFFICE: Margaret River Office, Bussell Highway, Margaret River, phone (09) 9757 2322.

Hardy Inlet. Photo – Jiri Lochman

Blackwood River Forests

Tall jarrah and marri forest, winding bush drives, spring wildflowers and a broad expanse of peaceful water are some of the attractions of the forest east of Margaret River.

The Blackwood River is the longest river in the South-West. From its headwaters in the Wheatbelt, it meanders more than 500 kilometres to its broad estuary at Augusta. On its course it flows through flat plains, steep forested valleys, tall jarrah and marri forest and picturesque farmland. A large area of forest adjoining the river is protected in a reserve.

The Blackwood is the river venue for the annual Blackwood Classic Boat Race. It is navigable by canoe, from upstream of Bridgetown all the way to Augusta.

RECREATION AREAS

In the western part of the jarrah forest, between Nannup and Alexandra Bridge, the river provides a tranquil setting for camping, picnicking, fishing, swimming or canoeing. Gravel forest roads, suitable for two-wheel-drive vehicles for most of the year, lead to a selection of secluded spots.

Popular camping spots include Sues Bridge and Wrights Bridge, on the Blackwood River, and Barrabup Pool, near Nannup on St Johns Brook. Toilets, fireplaces and tables are provided. These sites are also excellent canoeing areas. Bring your own drinking water. Please leave no trace of your visit.

On the outskirts of the town of Nannup is the Kondil Park recreation area. Kondil is the Aboriginal name for sheoak. It was so-named because sheoaks were milled here when the Barrabup Mill was operational. The mill closed in 1925, but old sheoak stumps can still be seen in the area. Here, two walktrails (the Sheoak Walk and the Casuarina Walk) meander through natural bushland of jarrah, marri, banksia, sheoak, paperbarks and blackboys. Wildflowers can be seen throughout the year, but September to November is the most impressive time.

Canoeing on the Blackwood. Photo – Dennis Sarson/Lochman Transparencies

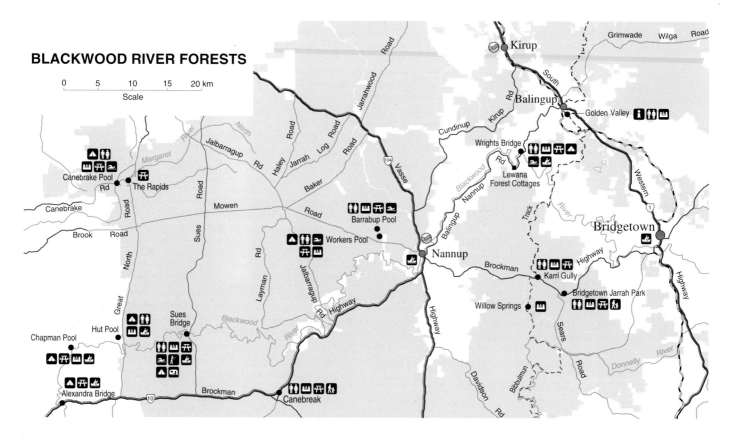

BLACKWOOD RIVER FORESTS

Between Nannup and Balingup is the old forestry settlement of Lewana. Nestled amongst a tranquil pine forest, five cottages are available for hire. The cottages are hidden in a lush forest valley near the Blackwood River. The expansive grounds of the settlement attract natural wildlife such as kangaroos and native birds. Barbecues, a playground, and tennis and volleyball facilities are provided on-site. The forest trails reveal spectacular panoramic views and enchanting waterfalls. Call (08) 9527 1844 to make bookings.

GOLDEN VALLEY AND OTHER PARKS

Just south of Balingup, a unique park for trees has been established. Called Golden Valley Tree Park, the picturesque valley features hundreds of tree species from Australia and overseas. The park provides a relaxing setting, with barbecues and picnic sites.

A park of a different kind can be found between Nannup and Bridgetown. Bridgetown Jarrah Park, on the Brockman Highway 25 kilometres west of Bridgetown, is an ideal place to discover the moods of Western Australia's remarkable jarrah forest. Meandering walktrails, on-site information and picnic facilities add to the enjoyment of the park.

Several other sites on the Margaret River and its tributaries, such as Canebrake Pool, provide alternatives to the sites on the Blackwood River.

When travelling in the Blackwood River forests, take care after rain, as some of the roads are prone to flooding. Some of this forest is closed to vehicles due to the risk of dieback. Drop in to one of the local CALM offices for the latest information on road conditions and fire hazards.

WHERE IS IT? Within a 50 km radius of Nannup.

TRAVELLING TIME: All sites lie less than an hour from Nannup.

WHAT TO DO: Camping, fishing, swimming, picnicking, canoeing, bushwalking.

WALKS:

Fallers Brand Trail, Bridgetown Jarrah Park: Medium 3.2 km, 1 hour walk meanders through Bridgetown Jarrah Park and commemorates the early days of the South-West timber industry.

Shield Tree Trail, Bridgetown Jarrah Park: This easy walk takes you to the Shield Tree, which harks back to the 1920s.

Sheoak Walk: 2 km, 1 hour loop through the Kondil Park recreation area near Nannup.

Casuarina Walk: 3 km, 1½ hour circuit through the Kondil Park recreation area near Nannup.

Timberline Trail: Medium, 15 km trail follows the old tramlines used to haul timber to the Barrabup Mill in the early 1900s. There are two remote campsites with views over the tranquil pools of St Johns Brook.

FACILITIES: Toilets, barbecues and tables.

NEAREST CALM OFFICES: Blackwood District Office is at South Western Highway, Kirup, phone (08) 9731 6232. The South West Capes District Office is at 14 Queen Street, Busselton, phone (08) 9752 1677.

FACING PAGE
Alexandra Bridge over the Blackwood River. Photo – Geoff Taylor/Lochman Transparencies

THE KARRI FOREST

Southern Ocean

| 10 | 8 | 6 | 4 | 2 | 0 | 5 | 10 | 15 | 20 km |

QUARRAM NATURE RESERVE

To Denmark and Albany

Peaceful Bay

Irwin Inlet

SEE PAGE 90

Conspicuous Beach

Valley of the Giants "Tree Top Walk"

Hilltop Road

Knoll Drive

Walpole Rd

Nth

Walpole

Sandy Beach

Isle Road

Newdegate Island

Sandy Island

Crystal Springs

Mandalay

Mount Clare

Nuyts Trailhead

Long Point

Cliffy Head

MT FRANKLAND NATIONAL PARK

Mt Frankland

Beardmore Rd

Fernhook Falls

Beardmore

Centre Road

Bibbulmun

Deeside Road

Chesapeake Road

Broke Inlet

Fish Creek

SHANNON NATIONAL PARK

Highway

Burnside

Shannon

SEE PAGE 82

Shanghai Gully

Snake Gully

Shannon River

Boorara Tree and Lane Poole Falls

Big Tree Grove

Curtin Rd

Coast Rd

Coast Road

Middleton Road

Western Road

Wheatley

Northcliffe

D'ENTRECASTEAUX NATIONAL PARK

Callcup Hill

Mt Chudalup

Windy Harbour

Gardner Beach

Coodamurrup Beach

Salmon Beach

Pt D'Entrecasteaux

LAKE MUIR NATURE RESERVE

Highway

Byenup Lagoon

Tordit Gurrup Lagoon

Lake Muir

Chindilup Pool

Boyndaminup

Strachan

Thomson

Bevan

Deep

Frankland

Kent River

Muirs Highway

Mordalup

Unicup

Lake Unicup

PERUP NATURE RESERVE

Perup Forest Ecology Centre

Old Heartlea Settlement

To Boyup Brook

Boyup

Tone Bridge

Brook

Cranbrook

Wingebellup

Kolonup Road

Frankland Road

Frankland

Rocky Gully Rd

Rocky Gully

To Mt Barker

Nornalup

Gordon River

Tone River

Terrace Road

To Bunbury

King Jarrah

Manjimup

Diamond Tree

South Western Highway

Donnelly

Graphite Rd

One Tree Bridge

Glenoran Pool

Sears Road

Davidson Rd

Donnelly Mill (Wheatley Dam)

Greens Island

Tom's Rd Crossing

Four Aces

Chappels Bridge Palings Camp Site

BEEDELUP NATIONAL PARK

Beedelup Falls

WARREN NP

Founders Forest

Pemberton

Gloucester Tree

East Brook

Moons Crossing

Brockman Saw Pits

SEE PAGE 89

Heartbreak Trail

Heartbreak Crossing

Yeagarup Lake

Ritter Rd

Warren River

Nannup

Vasse Highway

Donnelly Boat Landing

Jasper Beach

Yeagarup Beach

Warren Beach

To Nannup

Stewart Road

Canebreak

Brockman Hwy

To Augusta

Black Point

GINGILUP SWAMPS NATURE RESERVE

Lake Jasper

Blackwood River

Miyeannup

Coast Road

Chudalup

The Karri Forests

Manjimup to Walpole

Between Manjimup, Nannup and Denmark, deep in the cool well-watered South-West, grows one of the world's most magnificent forests. Towering karri trees, which rise to heights of 85 metres, and gnarled marri dominate the landscape. Cool rivers flow amongst the giant trees, and on the coast forest streams give way to estuaries and windswept heathlands.

Near Manjimup, areas such as One Tree Bridge provide a pleasant karri forest setting for picnics and bushwalks, while the nearby Donnelly River offers swimming, canoeing and fishing.

Pemberton is the heart of the big karri forest, and there are dozens of secluded picnic spots in the surrounding forests. The Warren River, its tributaries and several other free-flowing streams offer some of the best trout fishing in the State. Gloucester, Warren and Beedelup national parks, near Pemberton, protect representative or particularly scenic areas of karri forest.

On the coast, D'Entrecasteaux National Park covers 118 000 hectares of sweeping beaches, wild coastal wetlands and dunes, and offers superb beach fishing. Access is possible with a four-wheel-drive.

Near Walpole, in the south, Walpole-Nornalup National Park protects forested wilderness, coastal scenery and plant communities and animals typical of the region. Nornalup Inlet, and the Frankland and Deep Rivers, which flow through the national park, provide the setting for boating and fishing. Fifteen kilometres west of Denmark, William Bay National Park protects coastline, heath and karri forest, but is best known for its swimming beaches and coastal fishing.

Park access and roads in the region are generally graded gravel and suitable for conventional vehicles. Some four-wheel-drive tracks are shown on the maps. For your own safety, don't travel on log haulage roads, as logging trucks loaded with tonnes of timber travel at high speed along these broad gravel roads. These roads are signposted.

View of karri forest from Mt Frankland. Photo – Jiri Lochman

Manjimup

Manjimup is the heart of the southern timber industry, and was one of the first towns established in the region. The history of settlement and timber cutting can be followed in the town's Timber Park and Museum, but there are also many traces in the surrounding forests.

Donnelly Mill Village, set amongst karri forest on the banks of the Donnelly River, has been restored as a holiday village. East of Manjimup, huts at the old forestry settlement of Tone River are available for hire. Contact the Ministry of Sport and Recreation for more information.

The One Tree Bridge and Glenoran Pool recreation site on Graphite Road is surrounded by big karri. Fish for trout in the Donnelly River, picnic, or take one of the walktrails that wind through the trees and breathe in the atmosphere. Downstream, Glenoran Pool provides a quiet forested setting for a day trip.

Diamond Tree, a fire lookout built in 1939 which is still used, makes up a trilogy of karri tree towers which are open to the public, together with Gloucester Tree and Bicentennial Tree, both near Pemberton. Another forest giant worth visiting is the king jarrah tree near Manjimup, over two metres in girth.

Which tree is which? *Common Trees of the South-West Forests*, one of the many low-cost, full colour **Bush Books** published by the Department of Conservation and Land Management, will help you tell them apart.

WHERE IS IT? 35 km radius of Manjimup.

TRAVELLING TIME: No more than 1 hour

WHAT TO DO: Picnicking, bushwalking, birdwatching, fishing, canoeing, sightseeing, scenic driving.

FACILITIES:

Donnelly Mill Village: Barbecues, tables.

One Tree Bridge: Toilets, barbecues, picnic shelters.

WALKS:

Bibbulmun Track: Medium and longer walks along the newly-aligned Bibbulmun Track, a long distance walktrail between Perth and Albany, are available. Brochures and maps can be purchased showing where the track runs.

Jim Fox Adventure Trail, Diamond Tree: Easy 500 m walk. Fun for kids.

King Jarrah Trail: Easy 650 m, 15 minute trail. Access for wheelchairs. Interpreted with signs.

One Tree Bridge to Four Aces Trail: Easy 2 km, 40 minute scenic walk allows you to explore One Tree Bridge, the Four Aces and the towering forests in between. The northern part of the loop track is steep as it descends into the Donnelly Valley.

Maxwell Track: Moderate 5½ hour, 14 km return (or 7 km one way) walk through jarrah and flooded gum communities adjacent to the Tone River, between the Tone River Settlement and Chindilup Pool. It is recommended as a day walk. To halve the walk, you can have someone meet you at Chindilup Pool with a vehicle.

NEAREST CALM OFFICE: Manjimup District Office, Brain Street, Manjimup, phone (08) 9771 1988.

Chindilup Pool on the Tone River. Photo – Jiri Lochman

Perup Forest Ecology Centre

Perup Forest, about 56 kilometres north-east of Manjimup, is possibly the best location for viewing rare mammals in Australia. Perup is home to more species of mammal than any similar-sized area in the south of Western Australia. These include several rare and threatened species such as tammar wallabies, chuditch, quendas (southern brown bandicoots) and western ringtail possums.

The largest existing population of the woylie, estimated to be more than 5 000 animals, lives in the area. Perup is also the only mainland location in Australia where tammar wallabies can be found. Woylies and tammar wallabies can usually be seen at dusk from carefully constructed 'hides' built to ensure that the animals are not disturbed by visitors. After dark, visitors can then participate in 'spotlighting' tours to view the mainly nocturnal wildlife. Perup is also a great place for birdwatching, with more than 80 species recorded there. A number of walktrails that lead from the lodge are ideal for early morning birdwatching.

Visitors to Perup can stay at the Perup Wilderness Lodge, set in State forest surrounded by the Perup Nature Reserve, which is the State's largest jarrah forest nature reserve.

The lodge has been built using rammed earth and has several environmentally sensitive features designed to maximise renewable resources. Drinking and shower water are collected from rain and all rubbish is taken off-site. The lodge is available for use by groups, but these must be accompanied by a CALM officer. A limited number of commercial tour operators have also been trained and licensed to use the lodge without being accompanied by CALM staff.

WHERE IS IT? 56 km from Manjimup.

TRAVELLING TIME: About 45 minutes drive from Boyup Brook, Manjimup or Bridgetown, around 1½ hours from Bunbury, and 3½ hours drive from Perth.

TOTAL AREA: The centre is on 100 ha of State forest, surrounded by the 52 000 ha Perup Nature Reserve.

ACCOMMODATION: Available on a twin share or single basis, and can cater for a maximum of 20 people (twin share) or 10 people (single occupancy).

WHAT TO DO: Night viewing of rare mammals in the wild, plus a range of bushwalks.

FACILITIES: The lodge is available on a self catering basis and has a fully equipped kitchen that is shared between the two buildings. Each building has its own ablution facilities.

HOW TO BOOK YOUR EXPERIENCE: Community and school groups should contact the Perup Booking Officer, CALM Manjimup District Office, phone (08) 9771 7988, fax (08) 9771 2677. To join a tour, contact the Living Windows hotline on (08) 9721 7778.

NEAREST CALM OFFICE: Manjimup District Office, Brain Street, Manjimup, phone (08) 9771 1988.

Perup Wilderness Lodge. Photo – Cliff Winfield

Pemberton

Pemberton boasts lush green karri, jarrah and marri trees towering over dense undergrowth. One of the town's main attractions is the Gloucester Tree, which the adventurous can scale for a bird's eye view of the surrounding karri forest (see page 86).

Other attractions include several wineries, fine woodcraft galleries and studios, a trout hatchery and a marron farm. Pemberton's Karri Visitor Centre, in the Pemberton Tourist Centre complex in Brockman Street, is recommended to find out more about the forest. It incorporates a Pioneer Museum and the Karri Forest Discovery Centre, with a theatrette and audiovisual. A modest charge applies. You can also take a ride in a 1907 replica tram. It traverses towering karri and marri forests, crossing rivers and streams on rustic wooden bridges. The tram leaves twice daily for tours of 1½ hours, and a steam train runs in winter and spring.

Big Brook Dam was built in 1986 to supplement water supplies to Pemberton and the nearby trout hatchery. You can swim or fish in this scenic lake surrounded by lush karri forest, also a great picnic spot. A walktrail loops around the dam, passing through the Big Brook Forest. It is accessible to wheelchairs, prams, strollers and bicycles and has shelters and seats at rest points along the way.

THE RAINBOW TRAIL SCENIC DRIVE

The Rainbow Trail is a short drive from Pemberton. It leads from the Pemberton Trout Hatchery to Big Brook Arboretum via Big Brook Dam, along the banks of Lefroy Brook. Barbecues and toilet facilities are set amongst tall karri. After lunch, try fishing for rainbow trout in the dam, or take a canoe out on the water.

If you had taken the drive 75 or so years ago a very different scene would have greeted you. Tumbled logs and a charred and blackened expanse of earth and debris would have spread for hectares on either side of the trail. Between 1920 and 1928, the entire area was clearfelled, and steam locomotives hauled the giant karri logs to the State sawmill at Pemberton. Rainbow and Tramway trails, which are now part of the forest drive, were the railway formations over which the timber was hauled.

After all the millable timber had been removed, debris littered the forest floor. Sparks from a bush locomotive started a fierce wildfire which tore through the felled area. Karri trees left standing when the forest was logged took advantage of the fire and, after the ashes had cooled, shed thousands of seeds into the rich ashbed. The result is the forest you see today. This principle forms the basis of modern karri forest regeneration.

The Big Brook Arboretum, located on the Rainbow Trail, is perfect for rambles. This garden of international and interstate trees was planted more than 50 years ago to monitor their growth in karri country. They include the giant Californian redwood.

FOREST RECREATION

The permanent waters of the Warren River and the smaller streams offer trout and marron fishing, while the larger waterways present the opportunity for a canoeing adventure. Rapids, shallows and logs in the river make it difficult to use larger boats in the inland waters.

The Founders Forest, north-west of Pemberton, is another regeneration area. It was once cleared to grow wheat, but the project failed and the area was abandoned. The karri forest regenerated after a fire induced seed fall from the surrounding areas. It was dedicated as State forest 31 years later.

Historic tram on the Warren River Bridge. Photo – Jiri Lochman

WHERE IS IT? 335 km south of Perth, 31 km from Manjimup.

TRAVELLING TIME: 3-4 hours from Perth, 20 minutes from Manjimup.

WHAT TO DO: Bushwalking, fishing, swimming, canoeing.

FACILITIES: Accommodation, shopping and dining facilities. Sightseeing tours, tram rides, horseriding, Aboriginal cultural tours, guided trout fishing and four-wheel-drive tours are available. There are picnic tables, toilets and barbecues at Big Brook Dam.

WALKS:

Hatchery Trail: Easy 2 km walk leads from the far side of the Pemberton Pool to the trout hatchery.

Trevor's Trail: Easy 2.4 km walk from the far side of the Pemberton Pool.

Karri Heights: Easy 2.4 km walk.

Whistler Walk: Moderate 2 km walk starting from the bottom of Pump Hill.

Lefroy Trail: Moderate 2.1 km walk to Lefroy Brook starting from the bottom of Pump Hill.

Gloucester Tree Walk: Moderate 3 km walk from Pemberton townsite to the Gloucester Tree. The trailhead is outside the Tourist Centre.

Bibbulmun Track: Medium and longer walks along the newly-aligned Bibbulmun Track, a long distance walktrail between Perth and Albany, are available. Brochures and maps can be purchased showing where the track runs.

Big Brook Arboretum: Easy 1.2 km circuit walk from the barbecue site.

Big Brook Dam: This medium 4 km, 1 to 1½ hour walktrail loops around Big Brook Dam, passing through the Big Brook Forest. It is accessible to wheelchairs, prams and strollers and has shelters and seats at rest points along the way.

Founders Forest: Two short walks, one of 1 km, the other of 300 m.

NEAREST CALM OFFICE: Pemberton District Office, Kennedy St, Pemberton, phone (08) 9776 1207.

Top right: Walktrails through tall karri forest. Photo – Len Stewart/Lochman Transparencies
Centre: Karri forest wildflowers. Photo – Cliff Winfield
Right: Bird hide at Big Brook. Photo – Cliff Winfield

Gloucester National Park

The Gloucester Tree, in Gloucester National Park, is probably Western Australia's most famous karri tree. This 60 metre high giant towers above the forest surrounding Pemberton. In the past, foresters maintained a regular fire lookout from its lofty crown. Today, visitors climb to the cabin in its upper branches for sensational views of the surrounding karri forest.

The Gloucester Tree was one of eight lookout trees built between 1937 and 1952 in the karri forest. The construction of fire lookout towers in the tallest trees of WA's karri forest was a practical response to one of the most serious threats to forest communities in the South-West – fire.

BUILDING THE LOOKOUT

The Gloucester Tree lookout was built in 1947, in the highest of the tall karri trees near Pemberton. The floor of its cabin sits 58 metres above the ground. The tree was one of a group on a ridge overlooking the East Brook. Conveniently located just three kilometres from Pemberton, it gives a commanding view of the surrounding countryside.

The suitability of the tree as a lookout was verified by forester Jack Watson after an epic climb. Using climbing boots and a belt to scale the tree, it took him six hours to reach a height of 58 metres and return. The ascent was made more difficult by the massive girth of the tree, some 7.3 metres, and the fact that limbs had to be negotiated from 39.6 metres. This is claimed to be a record climb, and is widely recognised in forestry circles as one of the greatest efforts of courage and endurance in the Australian forest.

The pegging of the ladder, and the lopping of the branches, was carried out by another legendary south-western forester, George Reynolds. During this work, a branch which he had cut through twisted in its fall and snapped off a number of pegs. George remained aloft for several hours while his assistant Len Nicol repegged the damaged section from below.

The construction of the lookout coincided with a visit to the South-West by the then Governor-General of Australia, His Royal Highness the Duke of Gloucester. A viewing of the operation was included in his itinerary and the royal party enjoyed a picnic in the bush and watched Reynolds at work. They were reportedly impressed with the cool manner he displayed while cutting through branches 40 centimetres in diameter, nearly 70 metres above the ground, with his razor-sharp axe. The lookout, and eventually also the national park, were subsequently named after the Duke.

CLIMBING THE TREE

Since its construction, the Gloucester Tree has captured the imagination of thousands of visitors to the karri country. A survey taken in 1963 revealed that 3 000 people had climbed the tree in that year. As its popularity continued to grow, the original wooden cabin was demolished in 1973 because its timber was deteriorating. It was replaced with a steel and aluminium cabin and visitors' gallery.

By 1990, the number of visitors to the Gloucester Tree had 'climbed' to about 223 000, of which 44 600 made it to the top. With the Dave Evans Bicentennial Tree, completed in 1988, and the Diamond Tree, built in 1939 and located 10 kilometres from Manjimup, it now makes up a trilogy of karri tree towers which are open to the public.

However, there is more to the Gloucester National Park than the lookout. One very popular recreation site nearby is The Cascades. Here, the Lefroy Brook tumbles over a series of rocky shelves, which vary from a gentle flow in mid-summer to a raging torrent in winter. These rocky rapids, set amid the karri forest at the southern end of Gloucester National Park, provide a place for an outdoor lunch, a leisurely afternoon stroll, or a few peaceful hours of fly fishing.

WHERE IS IT? About 3 km from Pemberton.

TRAVELLING TIME: 5 minutes from Pemberton.

TOTAL AREA: 875 ha.

WHAT TO DO: Bushwalking, fishing, tree climbing (visitor fees apply).

FACILITIES: Picnic tables, toilets, lookouts, barbecues at Gloucester Tree and The Cascades.

WALKS:

The Duke's Walk: Easy 400 m loop to view the karri forest at close quarters.

Gloucester Tree to Cascades: Hard 12 km return walk.

The Cascades: Easy 1.2 km, 30 minute loop crossing the Lefroy Brook and The Cascades.

Karri Views: Easy 800 m walk giving unparalleled views of karri forests.

Gloucester Route: Medium 10 km walk.

East Brook: Three walks have been constructed through the Gloucester National Park:

- **Nyoongar** - Easy 800 m, one way.
- **Waugals** - Easy 3 km, one way.
- **Gloucester** - Moderate 10 km.

NEAREST CALM OFFICE: Pemberton District Office, Kennedy St, Pemberton, phone (08) 9776 1207.

FACING PAGE
The Cascades of Lefroy Brook. Photo – Marie Lochman

Right: The famous Gloucester Tree. Photo – Jiri Lochman/CALM

Beedelup and Warren national parks

BEEDELUP NATIONAL PARK

Beedelup National Park is mostly karri forest, with some mixed forest. The park is adjacent to Karri Valley Resort, on the Vasse Highway west of Pemberton. Its major attraction is the Beedelup Falls, which are in full flow during winter and spring. You must descend the steep steps through a corridor of trees to reach the first bridge of the falls. The falls can be viewed along a walktrail, sections of boardwalk and from two bridges.

WARREN NATIONAL PARK

Warren National Park is in the heart of the karri forest, south-west of Pemberton on the Old Vasse Road. It protects magnificent virgin karri forest along the valley of the Warren River. However, the roads are steep and rough, and not suitable for buses or vehicles towing caravans or trailers.

The one-way Heartbreak and Maidenbush trails follow the Warren River. The river is flanked by magnificent karri trees, river banksias, peppermints and the wattie (*Agonis juniperina*). The rapids of Heartbreak Crossing and the Warren Lookout are good places to stop along the trail.

The park is also home to some of the largest karri trees, including the Dave Evans Bicentennial Tree, one of the fire lookout trees.

WHERE ARE THEY? The parks lie within a 15 km radius of Pemberton. Fees must be paid to enter both parks.

TRAVELLING TIME: 10 minutes from Pemberton.

TOTAL AREA: Beedelup National Park covers 1 786 ha and Warren National Park is 2 982 ha.

WHAT TO DO: Swimming, camping, bushwalking, canoeing, fishing.

FACILITIES: Beedelup National Park has a boardwalk and bridges. At Warren National Park there is a covered picnic and barbecue area, free gas and wood barbecues, toilets and water.

WALKS:

Beedelup Falls: This 600 m walk should not be missed.

Bicentennial Tree to Warren Lookout: Easy 2.4 km, 1 hour return walk through huge old growth karri forest in Warren National Park.

NEAREST CALM OFFICE: Pemberton District Office, Kennedy St, Pemberton, phone (08) 9776 1207.

FACING PAGE
Lookout at Warren National Park. Photo – Dennis Sarson/Lochman Transparencies
Below: Beedelup Falls. Photo – Jiri Lochman

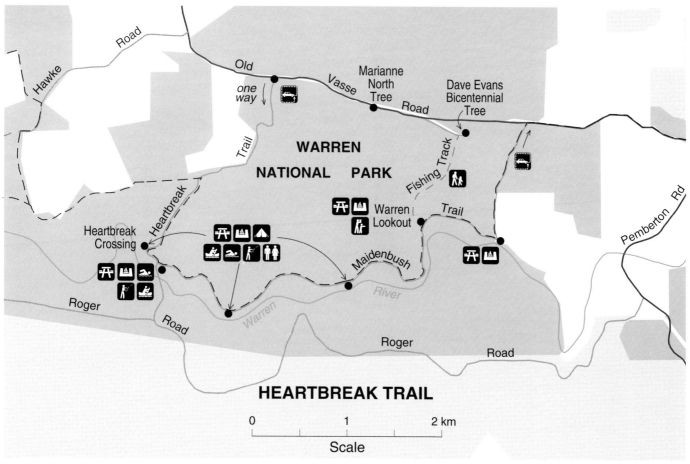

HEARTBREAK TRAIL

0   1   2 km

Scale

D'Entrecasteaux National Park

Spectacular coastal cliffs, pristine beaches, mobile sand dunes, and even pockets of karri are all part of the scenery at D'Entrecasteaux National Park. The park has isolated beach camp sites, wild coastal vistas and excellent fishing. Few facilities are provided throughout the park. The town of Northcliffe lies only eight kilometres from the park and is en route to delightful spots at Mount Chudalup and Salmon Beach.

Major streams and rivers, including the Warren, Donnelly and Shannon, drain through D'Entrecasteaux and empty into its coastal waters. High sand dunes and limestone cliffs on the sea coast give way to coastal heathlands and a series of lakes and swamps further inland. These include Lake Yeagarup and Lake Jasper, which is the largest freshwater lake in the southern half of WA. An area of wetlands behind the coastal dunes is known as The Blackwater. Another outstanding feature is the Yeagarup Dune, an impressive mobile dune 10 kilometres long.

The national park also surrounds one of WA's largest inlets. Broke Inlet is also the only large estuary in the South-West that has not been significantly altered, either by developments along its shores or within its catchment area. Lying at the park's eastern end, it is a large, shallow estuary, linked to the ocean by a narrow channel that passes through high ridges of windblown sand dunes. Sandy beaches along its shores are interspersed with low, rocky headlands, with numerous small islands offshore. The bulk of the catchment area of this serene body of water is protected in the adjacent Shannon National Park (see page 92).

The basalt columns west of Black Point, a popular fishing and surfing spot, have created one of the park's most stunning landforms. This feature originated from a volcanic lava flow, some 135 million years ago. The formation resulted from the slow cooling of a deep pool of lava, similar to the development of mud cracks. In the process of it cracking and shrinking, a close-packed series of hexagonal columns were formed. They are now slowly being eroded by the sea.

RECREATION

Windy Harbour, Salmon Beach, Mandalay Beach and Broke Inlet are the only coastal areas of this large park which are accessible by conventional vehicle. Four-wheel-drive tracks lead to other coastal fishing and camping spots. Stay on existing tracks and let your tyres down to cope with sand. Sand tracks make travelling slow inside the park. Many places, such as the mouth of the Donnelly River, can be reached only by small boat. Significant vehicle exclusion areas provide those who are willing to hike with an opportunity to experience seclusion on a deserted beach.

There is a campground at Lake Jasper with shaded campsites, barbecues, picnic tables, water and toilets. If you intend to go walking make sure you are properly equipped with a map, compass and water – this is wild country.

WHERE IS IT? The park stretches for 130 km, from Black Point (35 km east of Augusta) to Long Point west of Walpole, extending inland for between 5 and 20 km. It lies 8 km from Northcliffe and 40 km from Pemberton.

TRAVELLING TIME: Sand tracks make travelling slow within the park.

TOTAL AREA: 116 668 ha.

WHAT TO DO: Camping, bushwalking, boating, fishing, beachcombing.

FACILITIES: Camping area with barbecues, picnic tables, water and toilets at Lake Jasper; barbecues at Mount Chudalup, barbeques and toilets at Salmon Beach; lookouts and boardwalk at Mandalay Beach. Fresh water, toilets and barbecue facilities are provided in a pleasant campsite at Crystal Springs, near Walpole, under a stand of peppermint trees.

WALKS:

Mount Chudalup: Scenic, moderate to steep, but not overly strenuous 1 km, 30 minute walk to the top of Mount Chudalup.

NEAREST CALM OFFICES: Pemberton District Office, Kennedy St, Pemberton, phone (08) 9776 1207.

FACING PAGE
Cathedral Rock near Windy Harbour in D'Entrecasteaux National Park. Photo – Jiri Lochman

Red swamp banksia (Banksia occidentalis). Photo – Cliff Winfield/CALM

GINGILUP SWAMPS
NATURE RESERVE

BEEDELUP
NATIONAL PARK

Channybearup Road

Diamond Tree

Founders
Forest

Big Brook Dam

WARREN
NP

Beedelup Falls

Black Point

Jasper Beach

Lake Jasper

Donnelly Boat
Landing

Donnelly River

Nasse

South Highway

East Brook

Pemberton

Warren River

Mordalup Road

Lake Unicup

Muirs

Strachan

Chindilup
Pool

Boyndaminup Highway

Lake
Muir

Heartbreak
Trail

Ritter Rd

Brockman
Saw Pits

Moons
Crossing

Western Road

Great Forest Trees Drive

Curtin Rd

Coast Road

Bevan Road

Heartbreak Crossing

Yeagarup Lake

Yeagarup Beach

Warren Beach

Callcup Hill

4WD

Warren

D'ENTRECASTEAUX
NATIONAL PARK

Middleton Road

Northcliffe

259

Wheatley Trk

Snake Gully

Big Tree Grove

Shannon

SEE PAGE 92

Shanghai Gully

Shannon River

SHANNON
NATIONAL PARK

Deeside Road

Highway

MT FRANKLAND
NATIONAL PARK

Thomson

Boorara Tree and
Lane Poole Falls

Southern Ocean

Summertime

Mt Chudalup

Salmon Beach

Pt D'Entrecasteaux

Windy Harbour

Sandy Island

Gardner Beach

Coodamurrup Beach

Gardner River

Chesapeake Trk

Moores

Broke Inlet Rd

Bibbulmun Track

Shannon Road

Broke Inlet

Fernhook Falls

Beardmore Rd

Nth

Walpole Rd

Fish Creek

Burnett

Centre
Road

Crystal
Springs

Mandalay

Mount Clare

Nuyts Trailhead

Cliffy Head

Long Point

Walpole

Irwin
Inlet

Sandy
Beach

Newdegate
Island

**D'ENTRECASTEAUX
NATIONAL PARK**

0   5   10   20   30 km

Scale

Shannon National Park

Shannon National Park is set in some of the most magnificent karri country in WA's southern forest. Within easy driving distance of the charming town of Northcliffe, the park covers the entire basin of the Shannon River and boasts giant forest trees, delicate orchids, paperbark swamps, some ancient wildlife and granite outcrops rising like islands above the sea of trees.

HISTORY

Shannon was one of the last areas in the South-West to be opened up for logging, due to its inaccessibility. The area was largely untouched until the 1940s, when there was an acute shortage of timber after the Second World War. Timber cutting began in the Shannon basin in the mid-1940s, and the town and timber mill were established in the late 1940s.

The information shelter at Shannon is near the site of the old mill. The town was built across the highway where the camping ground now stands. The settlement was designed for 90 mill houses in a double horseshoe

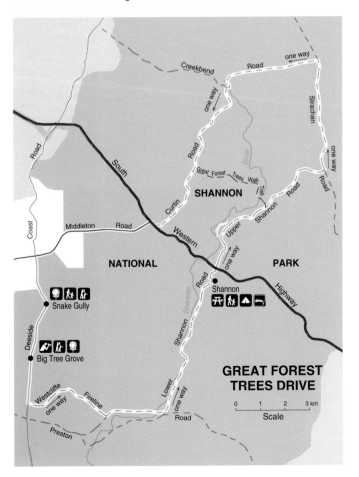

surrounding the area, which eventually included a hall, church, store, post office and nursing station. A dam was built upstream from the mill site in 1949 to ensure summer water supplies. The picturesque location meant it also became a popular swimming and marroning spot.

After Shannon Mill closed, the houses from the old townsite were sold and taken away. Today, only a few traces of the mill town and former forestry settlement can be seen, such as the fruit trees still growing in cleared areas of the Shannon camping ground. You can also see the remains of old buildings and railway lines along the Shannon Dam walktrail. Old logging tramways and roads are now used for walktrails and scenic drives. The area was gazetted as a national park in December 1988.

GREAT FOREST TREES DRIVE

The Great Forest Trees Drive was established in 1996. This 48 kilometre drive takes in stunning old growth karri forest, and is punctuated with six picnic and information stops, and two walks. It takes in stunning examples of marri and jarrah forest, sedgeland, heath and granite outcrops. The drive starts north of the South Western Highway, just beyond the shingled roof information shelter and the turn-off to the covered barbecue areas and walktrails. Before proceeding, visitors can read the information at the shelter, walk to the dam or have a barbecue lunch.

The roads for the drive are not sealed, but are suitable for conventional vehicles and small coaches. Great Forest Trees Drive signs show the way from the information shelter onto Upper Shannon Road and indicate where visitors should tune in their car radios to hear broadcasts about the area on a special park radio circuit.

After following the one-way northern loop for 23 kilometres, the drive crosses the highway into the lower Shannon area, where the roads are once again two-way. After visiting Snake Gully Lookout and Big Tree Grove, where you can see karri giants, the drive returns along the river to the old Shannon townsite. The loop ends where it begins, on the South Western Highway.

THE SHANNON LODGE

Adjacent to the camping area, the Shannon Lodge is available for group accommodation, and can sleep up to six people. It has single beds, hot water, a toilet and a slow combustion stove. You can book this facility by contacting CALM's Pemberton office.

WHERE IS IT? 33 km east-north-east of Northcliffe, 53 km south-east of Manjimup and 67 km from Walpole.

TRAVELLING TIME: 30 minutes from Northcliffe, 45 minutes from Manjimup and Walpole, 30 minutes from Pemberton.

TOTAL AREA: 53 500 ha.

WHAT TO DO: Camping, bushwalking, picnicking, canoeing, fishing.

Great Forest Trees Drive: This 48 km drive through spectacular old growth karri forest starts north of the South Western Highway.

FACILITIES: Barbecues, picnic tables, toilets and information panels.

Below right: The Shannon/Broke Inlet. Photo – Cliff Winfield

WALKS:

The Rocks Walktrail: Medium 5.5 km, 2 hour trail through tall forest to a granite outcrop overlooking the old Shannon townsite.

Shannon Dam Trail: Easy 3.5 km, 1½ hour return walk. The first 1.5 km is suitable for wheelchairs.

Great Forest Trees Walk: Medium 8 km, 3 hour return walk connects the arms of the one-way northern loop of the Great Forest Trees Drive. The walk follows an old forestry track and is steep in places, particularly where the trail crosses the Shannon River. In winter, the Shannon may burst its banks, and sometimes cut the track. Begins at the trailhead sign, 3.9 km north of the Shannon campsite.

USEFUL CALM PUBLICATIONS: *Great Forest Trees Drive, Shannon National Park* (a map and drive guide).

NEAREST CALM OFFICE: Pemberton District Office, Kennedy St, Pemberton, phone (08) 9776 1207.

Mount Frankland National Park

Mount Frankland National Park offers breathtaking views of the surrounding karri, tingle and jarrah forests. The park is exceptionally good for viewing forest wildflowers during late spring.

An easy 1.5 kilometre walktrail leads through tall karri and marri trees, with a lush understorey that includes tassel bush (*Leucopogon*), bracken fern, green kangaroo paws, white clematis (*Clematis pubescens*) and snottygobble trees (*Persoonia longifolia*). The path then traverses a boardwalk over the bare granite and makes its way around the base of Mount Frankland, through beautiful karri forest sprinkled with wildflowers. The views are delightful (see the photo on page 81), and the path is quite an easy grade. It will return you direct to the car park.

A trail branches off to climb the steep path to the top of this granite monadnock. After passing a sheer, mossy face of granite, narrow concrete steps wind steeply upward, through small pockets of soil and vegetation. Bullich (*Eucalyptus megacarpa*) grows alongside the steps. Like karri, this smooth-barked tree sheds its old grey bark to reveal mottled tonings of yellow, pink, orange, pale grey and white, but it does not grow as tall as karri and has much larger fruits.

You have to negotiate steep metal stairs to reach the summit of Mount Frankland, 411 metres above sea level. On top is an operational fire spotting tower. On a clear day you can see the Stirling and Porongurup ranges and to Chatham Island, near Walpole. The granite monadnock to the north is Mount Roe and the flat hill to its left is Mount Mitchell.

FERNHOOK FALLS

About 17 kilometres west of Mount Frankland, along Beardmore Road, is the Fernhook Falls camping area. It has a spectacular setting in State forest. Toilets, barbecue facilities, basic huts and a canoe launch area are provided. Camping fees apply.

WHERE IS IT? 27 km north of Walpole via North Walpole Road and Mt Frankland Road. The road into the park is gravel, so please take care, as it can be quite corrugated and slippery in places.

TRAVELLING TIME: 30-40 minutes from Walpole.

TOTAL AREA: 30 830 ha.

WHAT TO DO: Camping, bushwalking, picnicking.

FACILITIES: Picnic tables, barbecues, toilets, drinking water, camping facilities, lookout.

WALKS:

Mount Frankland: Medium 1 km return, 30 minute walk to the summit. You must negotiate concrete steps and a ladder to climb to the top. Well worth it!

Rockwood Trail: Easy 1.5 km, 30 minute loop around the base of Mount Frankland.

NEAREST CALM OFFICE: Walpole District Office, South Western Highway, Walpole, phone (08) 9840 1027.

Frankland River. Photo – Jiri Lochman

FACING PAGE
Mt Frankland provides walks with spectacular views. Photo – Cliff Winfield

Walpole

The star attractions of Walpole are its stunning inlets. The town overlooks the shallow Walpole Inlet, which is fed by the freshwater Walpole River. Nornalup Inlet is larger and deeper (up to five metres) and fed by the freshwater Deep River and the saltier Frankland River.

The estuaries are joined by a natural one kilometre long and two metre deep channel, bordered by steep granite hills and rocky shores. These are known locally as 'The Knolls' and are covered with dense karri forest. Other channels allow boats to navigate from the town jetty to the ocean bar. This is one of few inlet bars on the southern coast that remains open to the sea all year round. The estuaries are always tidal, salty and have both marine and estuarine fish. The open inlet mouth, the mixing of fresh and salt river waters, river deltas and two large inlets provides a great variety of marine habitats and a great range of fish. Black bream, whiting, trevally, herring and juvenile WA salmon are just a few of the 37 fish species that have been recorded here.

Former Premier Sir James Mitchell, a holiday-maker to these parts in the 1920s, closed the inlets to professional fishers and net fishing. This is still the case today. The long-standing ban on net fishing has helped to conserve estuarine fish stocks and has contributed to the excellent recreational fishing opportunities found in the inlets today.

Keep an eye open for the pelican, black swan, black duck and grey teal, which use the waters as a stopover, while the white-breasted sea eagle uses the tall karri on the knolls to build a nest and survey fishing prospects.

The Nornalup and Walpole estuaries form the only permanently open estuarine system of the South-West that is surrounded by predominantly forested national park. It is one of the State's most spectacular estuarine environments.

HISTORY

Sealers and whalers were the first Europeans to arrive on Walpole's coast in the early 1800s. Their glowing reports of sheltered inlets, huge trees and great deep rivers brought William Preston and his party to officially explore the Walpole-Nornalup area in 1837. Four years later, William Nairn Clark and his party rowed into Nornalup and described the areas around the Deep River and the Frankland River. According to his diaries:

> 'The sail up was truly delightful. The river actually appeared to be embosomed amongst lofty wooded hills, with tall eucalypt trees close to the water's edge, and crowning the summits of these high hills thus casting a deep gloom over the water and making the scenery the most romantic I ever witnessed in the other quarters of the globe.'

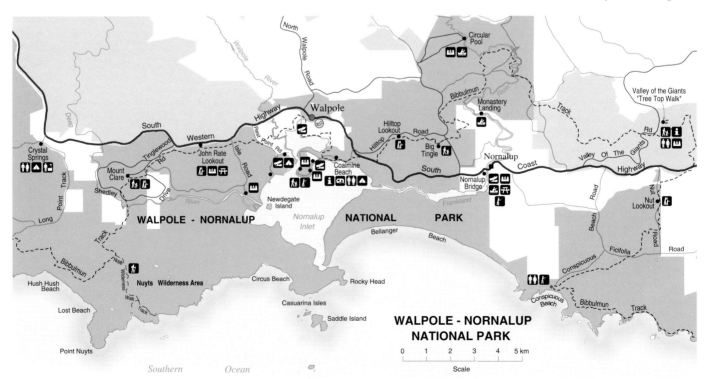

WALPOLE - NORNALUP
NATIONAL PARK

0 1 2 3 4 5 km

Scale

In 1845, a group of Englishmen, led by Henry Landor, set up a camp on Newdegate Island, at the delta of the Deep River. They planned to catch and salt fish for export and graze cattle and horses. Within a year the venture failed. In the 1850s, settlers from further inland began to drive cattle down to coastal areas in the present national park for summer grazing. Stock camps were established along the coast. Part of one camp can still be found at Crystal Springs.

Permanent settlement began in 1910, when Frenchman Pierre Bellanger and his family took up land beside the Frankland River. The next year, an English family, the Thompsons, settled at Deep River.

The rest of the district was opened up for agriculture through land settlement schemes in 1924, 1927 and 1930. The settlement, a scheme of then Premier Sir James Mitchell, was designed to foster a flourishing agricultural community that would contribute to the rural economy of WA and create livelihoods for unemployed men and their families. The original town, on what is now Pioneer Park, began as a tent, tin and bush pole shanty, in 1930. At first called Nornalup, the name was changed to Walpole in 1934.

Those attracted to the scheme lived in a makeshift main camp, until blocks of 120 acres (47.6 hectares) of forested land were allocated to each by ballot. Then began the hard work of clearing, fencing, building a more permanent home and carving an existence from the land. However, infertile land, indomitable forests, lack of farming skills and the hardship of the 1930s depression beset the settlement. Of the 100 blocks balloted, 85 were settled and less than a third of the original families stayed on.

Top: Point Nuyts. Photo – Cliff Winfield
*Above right: Red-flowering gum (*Corymbia ficifolia*). Photo – Len Stewart/Lochman Transparencies*

WHERE IS IT? 420 km south of Perth.

TRAVELLING TIME: 5 hours.

WHAT TO DO: Camping, bushwalking, fishing, four-wheel-driving, canoeing, swimming, picnicking, scenic driving.

FACILITIES: Accommodation, shops and restaurants. Estuary cruises and four-wheel-drive tours are available.

USEFUL CALM PUBLICATIONS: *Discovering the Valley of the Giants and Walpole-Nornalup National Park.*

NEAREST CALM OFFICE: Walpole District Office, South Western Highway, Walpole, phone (08) 9840 1027.

Walpole-Nornalup National Park

Think you've seen a forest? How about standing inside a living tree trunk or high among the branches, watching birds fly *below* you? You can do both at the Valley of the Giants in the tingle forest of Walpole-Nornalup National Park. As well as being a place of immense variety, Walpole-Nornalup National Park is home to four rare and wonderful trees – the red, yellow and Rate's tingles, and the red-flowering gum.

Walpole-Nornalup National Park surrounds the Walpole and Nornalup Inlets, and the rivers that run into them meander through dramatic changes in the landscape. High cliffs of limestone and granite are backed by dunes. Inland, on the southern edge of the great plateau of Western Australia, granite hills and ridges rise up to 100 metres above the surrounding swampland. In the south-west of the park, about 5 000 hectares of near-pristine bushland has been set aside for bushwalkers seeking wild solitude and beauty.

TREE TOP WALK AND ANCIENT EMPIRE TRAIL

The Valley of the Giants Tree Top Walk is an exhilarating walk through the canopy of the spectacular giant tingle trees in the Walpole-Nornalup National Park. The 'giants' are unique red tingle trees – the most massive of all eucalypts. They reach up to 60 metres tall and can have huge hollowed trunks up to 20 metres in circumference.

The Tree Top Walk provides an exciting and different perspective on the shapes, sounds and movement of the rare tingle forest. This is the world's only such walk in tall eucalypt forest with a rigid structure. It comprises a series of lightweight bridge spans, each 60 metres long and four metres deep, supported between pylons. The walkway rises with no steps, on a gentle grade suitable for kids, wheelchairs and the elderly, up to 40 metres above the forest floor, where it crosses a valley. There is a charge for going on the Tree Top Walk.

At ground level, the Ancient Empire Trail allows people to explore the science, fantasy, intrigue and grandeur of the old trees. A universally accessible boardwalk with wide paths, stable surfaces, no steps and gentle gradients takes people to one of the most popular of the gnarled veterans. The second section is a mixture of boardwalk and rammed earth path, which winds in and out, up, over and through seven more giants. Contemplative stops are scattered along the way, with seats and thought-provoking poetry sculpted into metal leaf structures. Amid the giant tingle trees one can find the smallest of worlds. Ferns, mosses and tiny delicate orchids also grow in the dense jungle-like understorey. Tiny fruiting fungi, in many shapes and colours, adorn the nooks and crannies of the tree trunks and forest floor.

THE TREES THAT TIME FORGOT

Part of the fascination of the tingle forest is the weird, almost primordial appearance of red tingle trees, with trunks like contorted faces. In fact, the tingle trees are caught in a botanical time warp of sorts. Research suggests that tingles were much more widespread during a past wetter era. But, after many thousands of years of diminishing rainfall, their distribution has contracted to just a few thousand hectares around Walpole, which has the wettest and least seasonal climate in the South-West.

The tingle forest's invertebrate tenants have also survived a remarkable journey through space and time. They hark back from a time when the Australian continent was joined to Antarctica, India, Africa and South America to make up the supercontinent Gondwana.

Because of the wet climate and the persistence of the tingle trees, which provide a moist, protected habitat, a number of invertebrate species have been able to survive from these ancient times – and are today still found in Walpole-Nornalup National Park. They include the tingle spider (*Moggridgea tingle*) and other spider species (*Baalebulb* species and *Dardarnus* species), primitive snails, and the ancient *Peripatus*, which is a living link between worms and arthropods. Related species survive in the rainforests of Tasmania, eastern Australia, New Zealand, Chile and Madagascar, now far flung, but which were once united as Gondwana.

Descolea maculata, one of many species of fungi that help the larger plants take up nutrients, is a member of a genus of fungi that associates with southern beech, a species that has been extinct in WA for many thousands of years.

Coalmine Beach. Photo – Jiri Lochman

FACING PAGE
Tree Top Walk. Photo – Michael James/CALM

WHERE IS IT? Within a 20 km radius of Walpole.

TRAVELLING TIME: 1 hour.

TOTAL AREA: 15 861 ha.

WHAT TO DO: Camping, bushwalking, four-wheel-driving, canoeing, swimming, picnicking, scenic driving.

Hilltop - Circular Pool Scenic Drive: A 24 km loop (4 km sealed, 20 km gravel) drive through magnificent tingle and karri forest, with views to the coast and inlets, takes you to a large pool on the Frankland River with rocky rapids in winter.

FACILITIES: Large range of facilities at various recreation sites, including a Tree Top Walk and whale watch platform.

WALKS:

Valley of the Giants Tree Top Walk: Easy 600 m, 20 minute walk through the canopy of the giant tingle forest. Fees apply. Suitable for children, assisted wheelchairs and the elderly.

Valley of the Giants Ancient Empire Walk: Easy 400 m, 30 minute boardwalk and rammed earth trail over the tingle forest floor. Suitable for children, assisted wheelchairs and the elderly.

Hilltop Giant Tingle Tree Trail: Easy 800 m, 30 minute walk to a large, old tingle tree that has, over many years, been hollowed out by fire. Suitable for children, assisted wheelchairs and the elderly.

Coalmine Beach Heritage Trail: Medium, 6 km return, 2 hour walk from Walpole to Coalmine Beach, with interpretive plaques.

Conspicuous Cliff Walks: Easy walks take in outstanding views from a limestone knoll, beaches, rocky headlands and a whale watch platform. Lengths vary from 200 m to 800 m return.

Bibbulmun Track: Medium and longer walks along the newly-aligned Bibbulmun Track, a long distance walktrail between Perth and Albany, are available. Brochures and maps can be purchased showing where the track runs.

USEFUL CALM PUBLICATIONS: *Discovering the Valley of the Giants and Walpole-Nornalup National Park.*

NEAREST CALM OFFICE: Walpole District Office, South Western Highway, Walpole, phone (08) 9840 1027.

Top: Ancient Empire Trail. Photo – Michael James/CALM
Above: Purple enamel orchid. Photo – Jiri Lochman

William Bay National Park

This small but attractive park protects stunning coastline and forest between Walpole and Denmark. Take care when exploring, however, as there are unpredictable surges on the coast outside of Greens Pool.

COAST AND SCENERY

Granite boulders and rocky shelves form much of the coastline between Greens Pool and Madfish Bay, extending 100 metres or more out to sea, and creating a reef which bears the brunt of heavy seas. Inside the reef, sheltered pools, channels and granite terraces create a fascinating seascape for beachcombing. At Greens Pool, a sheltered swimming beach is extremely popular in summer.

On the coast, the granitic rocks are well weathered and rounded, providing spectacular coastal scenery and supporting a peculiar flora. The beach at William Bay is narrow, and the sand tossed up by winter storms blows inland to build up high coastal dunes. Some sand dunes have travelled a few kilometres inland, before being colonised by dense scrub and trees to form an undulating row of sandy hills parallel to the coast. At William Bay, bare, moving sand dunes are still actively burying living stands of karri forest and, as the sand moves, revealing the upper parts of majestic old karri trees, which were once covered by shifting sand.

William Bay has high hills of granitic rocks. Light grey, windswept tors give the hill tops a primeval appearance. At Tower Hill, unusual granite boulders and a patch of 60 metre tall karri forest create a striking landscape.

WHERE IS IT? 15 km west of Denmark. Approach via South Coast Highway and William Bay Road.

TRAVELLING TIME: 15 minutes from Denmark or 45 minutes from Albany.

TOTAL AREA: 1 867 ha.

WHAT TO DO: Swimming, beachcombing, snorkelling.

FACILITIES: A viewing platform overlooks the popular family beach and dramatic coastal scenery at Greens Pool. The lookout and nearby toilets are designed to give disabled people easy access. Camping is not permitted but accommodation is available at nearby Denmark.

NEAREST CALM OFFICE: The park has a resident ranger who lives at the main entrance on William Bay Road. The Walpole District Office is at South Western Highway, Walpole, phone (08) 9840 1027.

Elephant Rocks. Photo – Colin Kerr

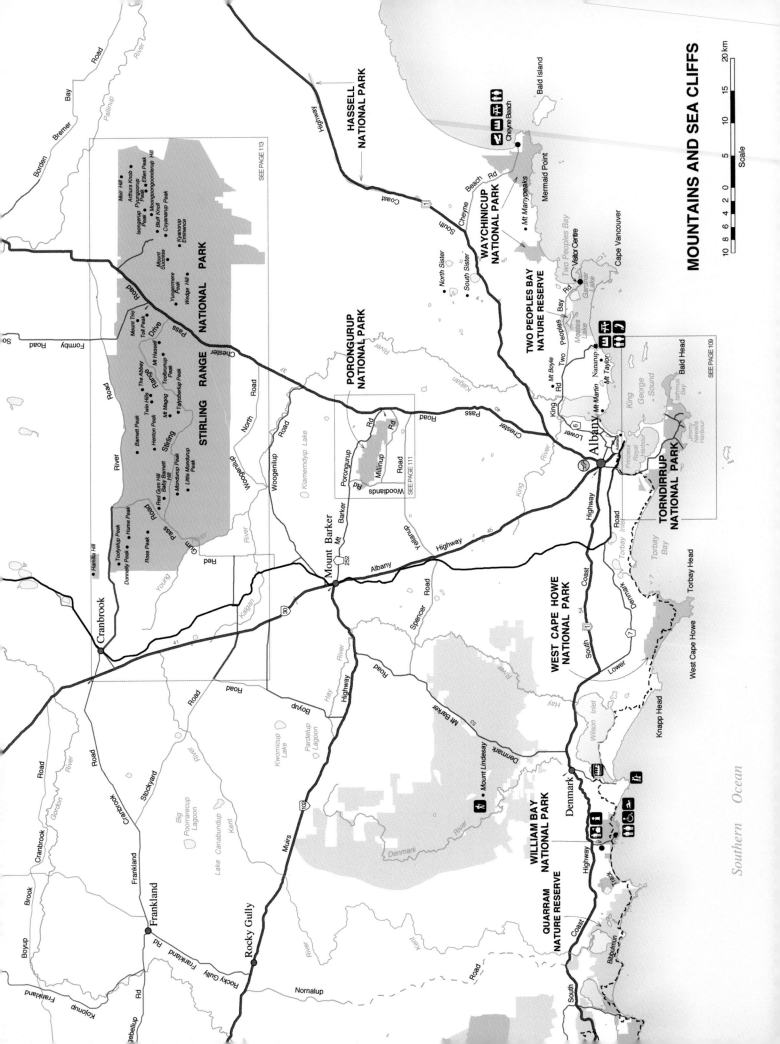

MOUNTAINS AND SEA CLIFFS

Scale
10 8 6 4 2 0   5   10   15   20 km

STIRLING RANGE NATIONAL PARK

Moir Hill
Arthurs Knob
Pyungurup Peak
Ellen Peak
Isongerup Peak
Moongoonderup Hill
Bluff Knoll
Coyanarup Peak
Kyanarup Eminence

Mount Success

Yungermere Peak
Wedge Hill

Mount Trio
Toll Peak

The Abbey
Mt Hassell
Bakers Knob
Toolbrunup Peak
Twin Hills
Herton Peak
Mt Magog
Talyuberlup Peak

Barnett Peak
Stirling

Red Gum Hill
Baby Barnett Hill
Mondurup Peak
Little Mondurup Peak

Toodyelup Peak
Hume Peak
Donnelly Peak
Ross Peak

Hamilla Hill

SEE PAGE 113

Cranbrook

PORONGURUP NATIONAL PARK

Porongurup Rd
Millinup Rd
Woodlands Road

SEE PAGE 111

Mount Barker
252

HASSELL NATIONAL PARK

North Sister
South Sister

WAYCHINICUP NATIONAL PARK

Cheyne Beach

Mermaid Point
Mt Manypeaks
Bald Island

TWO PEOPLES BAY NATURE RESERVE

Visitor Centre
Two Peoples Bay
Moates Lake
Gardner Lake
Cape Vancouver

Mt Boyle
King Rd
Mt Martin
Nanarup
Mt Taylor

Albany
9

King George Sound

Isthmus Bay
Bald Head
Jimmy Newells Harbour

SEE PAGE 109

Princess Royal Harbour

TORNDIRRUP NATIONAL PARK

Torbay Inlet
Torbay Bay
Torbay Head

WEST CAPE HOWE NATIONAL PARK

West Cape Howe
Knapp Head

Wilson Inlet

Denmark

WILLIAM BAY NATIONAL PARK

QUARRAM NATURE RESERVE

Blufulman

Mount Lindesay

Mount Barker

Frankland

Rocky Gully

Nornalup

Cranbrook

Southern Ocean

Borden
Bremer Bay
Pallinup River

Formby Road

Chester Pass Road

North Road
Woogenilup Road
Kojaneerup Lake
Red Gum Pass Road
Young River
Kalgan River

Albany Highway
Yellanup
King River
Kaljan River

Coast Road
Cheyne Beach Rd
South Coast Highway

Hay River
Denmark River
Kent River
Spencer Road

Muirs Highway

Boyup Brook
Kojonup
Gnowangerup

Frankland Road
Cranbrook Gordon River
Stockyard Road
Big Poorrarecup Lagoon
Lake Canabundup
Pardelup Lagoon
Kwornicup Lake

Rocky Gully Frankland Rd

Mountains & Sea Cliffs

Denmark to Albany

Rugged granite headlands, windswept heathland, sheltered bays and spectacular coastal scenery characterise the national parks and reserves of the Albany coast. A great variety of wildlife, vegetation and scenery is protected in these reserves, which form a vital network of refuges for native species in a land otherwise largely cleared for agriculture.

West of Albany, West Cape Howe National Park offers a wild and untouched coastal environment, with few facilities for visitors, while Torndirrup National Park near Albany, with its dramatic cliffs and rock formations, is easily accessible for day trips.

TAKE CARE

Even on calm days, unpredictable surges rising from the Southern Ocean, hundreds of kilometres away, may sweep over the shore. Because the edge of the continental shelf is so close to the coast at Torndirrup, the energy of these waves is not broken before they reach the shoreline. Don't risk being the next victim. Always watch the ocean, and stay well clear of the sea level.

To the east of Albany, the scenic Two Peoples Bay Reserve protects the endangered noisy scrub-bird, the Gilbert's potoroo and several other rare species.

Inland, the Porongurup National Park provides some picturesque settings for day visits and rambles amongst the State's more eastern karri forest, while 30 kilometres to the north the Stirling Range National Park, with its soaring peaks and unusual flowers and trees, provides a magnificent opportunity for a longer visit and longer hikes. If you intend to visit the back country, rock climb or hike overnight in the Stirling Range, always fill in the details for your party in the visitors' log books provided at Moingup Springs or at the Bluff Knoll picnic area. Water is limited throughout the Range, so take plenty with you.

Stirling Range panorama. Photo – Jiri Lochman

West Cape Howe National Park

A spectacular coastline, which includes the dolerite cliffs of West Cape Howe and the granite of Torbay Head, fronts the cold waters of the Southern Ocean at West Cape Howe National Park.

The cleared rural landscape and ringbarked trees of Torbay, near the park's entrance, are a vivid contrast to the shady karri forest just within the park boundary. The tall karri forest supports a dense understorey of tall shrubs – karri oak, karri hazel, karri wattle and the waterbushes. Where there is light and space, there are low shrubs of many blue-flowered species, such as tree hovea, dampiera and veronica.

Leaving the karri forest, less than a kilometre from the entrance, is just as startling as entering it. The vegetation drops to a low coastal heath within metres. Towards the coast, the landscape opens up and you may see Lake William, the largest of three freshwater lakes.

SCENIC GRANDEUR

As the road narrows and winds around the hills you can glimpse the ocean. To the east, the peninsula of Torndirrup National Park is abruptly terminated by Peak Head. Over the Southern Ocean lies Eclipse Island. Up the hill is a lookout, from which you can see the clean white sand of Shelley Beach curving beneath steep limestone hills, which drop sharply into the sea. The beach is bounded at both ends by huge granite boulders, formed at the same time as the granites of the Porongurup Range, 79 kilometres to the north. Across the water are Dunsky Head and Torbay Head, the southernmost point of Western Australia.

In spring, the park is a canvas of blazing colour. The striking reds of templetonias, vivid blues of thick-leaved fanflower (*Scaevola crassifolia*) and pinks of coastal banjine (*Pimelia ferruginea*) combine with the yellows of showy dryandra (*Dryandra formosa*) and candle banksia (*Banksia attenuata*). Dense clumps of peppermint grow as tall as the winds allow and are home to ringtail possums. These shy animals are only ever seen on a night walk through the park. The soft-leaved woollybush also stands in defiance of the wind. Beneath it, jacksonias, melaleucas and wattles form a dense shrub layer typical of the wind-pruned heathlands of the South Coast.

CLIFF HANGERS

At the last dune ridge, there are spectacular views of the Cape and the Southern Ocean. To the right, the coastline sweeps towards Bornholm Beach, famous for its salmon fishing, and on to William Bay National Park, 57 kilometres to the west. Ahead, the dark cliffs of West Cape Howe contrast with the muted colours of the granites and limestones in the rest of the park.

Four-wheel-drivers are urged to lower their tyre pressure to preserve the environment and improve their driving experience. The route to the Cape has several small tracks branching to the coast. The first of these winds to Golden Gates Beach, one of the area's best surfing spots. Others give access to rock fishing spots such as The Steps, which are among the best on the South Coast. Just before the cliffs, the vegetation changes abruptly, becoming lower and more sparse. The soil, derived from the black igneous dolerite rock which forms the Cape itself, also changes colour. The dolerite was squeezed up as molten rock from deep below the Earth's crust, and cooled below the surface, allowing the formation of relatively large crystals.

The cliffs of West Cape Howe plummet 75 metres into the sea, which pounds relentlessly at their base. The track continues towards Dunsky Beach, visible from the lookout above Shelley Beach. The short, sandy beach at the bottom of a steep hill is protected from the prevailing south-westerly winds.

Offshore, sponge-covered reefs provide the opportunity for divers to explore the rich marine life of the South Coast. New Zealand fur seals and Australian sea lions cruise along the shore in search of fish. Further out to sea, southern right whales, sometimes accompanied by their young, can be seen.

WHERE IS IT? About 30 km west of Albany. Approach via Cosy Corner Road, Coombes Road and Shelley Beach Road. Apart from the road to Shelley Beach, access is limited to four-wheel-drives and walkers.

TRAVELLING TIME: 35 minutes from Albany.

TOTAL AREA: 3 517 ha.

WHAT TO DO: Fishing, four-wheel-driving, bushwalking, rock climbing (for experienced climbers with proper equipment), hang gliding, scuba diving (beware of strong rip tides that sometimes occur in the area).

FACILITIES: Gas barbecue at Shelley Beach. There are two hang gliding platforms at Shelley Beach Lookout. Camping fees apply.

NEAREST CALM OFFICE: Rangers from Albany visit the park throughout the year. CALM's South Coast Regional Office is at 120 Albany Highway, Albany, phone (08) 9842 4500.

TAKE CARE ON THE COAST: This coastline has a notorious record for accidents and deaths, due to people being washed into the ocean by freak waves, gusting winds or extra large swells. Please exercise extreme caution and don't risk being the next victim.

FACING PAGE
Shelley Beach. Photo – Jiri Lochman

Albany

Breathtaking coastal scenery and magnificent marine life draw visitors to this beautiful town on the South Coast. As WA's first settlement, Albany is rich in history. It was granted 'city' status in 1998.

Middleton Beach and Ellen Cove are excellent swimming beaches with picnic, barbecue and playground facilities, while a steep winding road takes you to the top of Mount Clarence, with its commanding ocean and town views. Visitors will inevitably drive past a curious granite rock, which looks like a labrador and is aptly named Dog Rock.

HISTORIC ATTRACTIONS

The Albany Residency Museum offers information on the social and natural history of Albany and has a 'See and Touch Gallery'. It is a good place to start your visit to Albany. You can go on board the replica of the *Amity*, the sailing vessel which brought Albany's first settlers in 1826.

There is also plenty on offer for lovers of old buildings. The Old Farm at Strawberry Hill, off Middleton Road, was the site of the government farm for the settlement at Albany. It is managed by the National Trust and is open to visitors. The two storey stone building was constructed in 1836 to house the Government Resident, Sir Richard Spencer. Australia's first federal fortress, commissioned in 1893, is also open to visitors. The Princess Royal Fortress operated until 1956. There is also an Old Gaol, built in 1851 as the Convict Hiring Depot. The Anglican Church of St John the Evangelist was the first to be consecrated in WA, and the Old Post Office has been beautifully restored and contains an Inter-Colonial Communications Museum.

WHALE WATCHING

During the whale watching season, which lasts from about July to October each year, visitors can come eyeball to eyeball with southern right whales the size of a bus. They often come right inside Albany's Princess Royal Harbour. The whales may also be seen from vantage points on land. During summer, right whales prefer the open ocean, away from the coast, but during early winter and spring the cows come in close to shore. There, near the surf line in sheltered bays, they give birth to their young, before returning to deeper waters as summer approaches.

Southern right whales were sought after by whalers. In fact, they were called right whales because, in the days of open-boat whaling with hand harpoons, they were the 'right' ones to catch. They were slow-swimming, floated when dead, and yielded large amounts of valuable products — particularly oil for illumination and lubrication. Today, the population along the southern coast of Australia can be counted in the hundreds.

At Albany Whaleworld, near Frenchmans Bay, you can see relics from the days of this famous whaling town, such as the restored *Cheynes IV* whale chaser. Whaleworld is the world's only whaling museum created from an operational whaling station, which ceased operations in 1978. The attraction has a fascinating museum and regular guided tours. One of the reasons for its existence at Albany is the presence of sperm whales, which are deep sea animals, relatively close to the mainland in the Albany area.

OTHER UNDERWATER WONDERS

Amazing underwater seascapes are to be found in King George Sound and all around Albany's offshore islands and reefs. The wreck of the 42 metre long *Cheynes III* sits guard near the entrance of King George Sound, in 25 metres of water, providing a home to a huge variety of marine life. This former whaler is intact and provides divers with an awe-inspiring sight. Breaksea Island and Two Peoples Bay are among the area's other well-known dive sites. See CALM's book *More Dive & Snorkel Sites in Western Australia* for descriptions and mud maps.

WHERE IS IT? 403 km south-east of Perth, 54 km from Denmark.

TRAVELLING TIME: 5 hours drive from Perth, 40 minutes from Denmark.

WHAT TO DO: Whale watching, beachcombing, fishing, four-wheel-driving, bushwalking, scuba diving.

WALKS:

Possession Point Heritage Trail, Vancouver Peninsula: Moderate 2 hour, 4 km walk along the northern section of the peninsula.

There are numerous other walks in and around the town. See 'Coastal Walks around Albany' available from the Albany Tourist Bureau, Residency Museum or local CALM office.

FACILITIES: Full accommodation, shopping, dining and entertainment facilities. Scenic flights, sightseeing tours, dive and fishing charters, and four-wheel-drive safaris are available.

NEAREST CALM OFFICE: CALM's South Coast Regional Office is at 120 Albany Highway, Albany, phone (08) 9842 4500.

FACING PAGE
Top right: View of Albany. Photo – Dennis Sarson/Lochman Transparencies
Below right: The old farm, Strawberry Hill. Photo – Bill Belson/Lochman Transparencies

Torndirrup National Park

At Torndirrup National Park, the Southern Ocean has sculpted a Natural Bridge in the coastal granites and formed The Gap, where the waves rush in and out with tremendous ferocity. The Blowholes, a crackline in the granite, 'blows' air and occasionally spray, making an impressive noise as it does so. Windswept coastal heaths give way to massive granite outcrops, sheer cliffs and steep sandy slopes and dunes.

The area was one of the first in the State to be gazetted as a national park, in 1918, though it was not named until 1969 and only acquired a resident ranger in 1973. Torndirrup was the name of the Aboriginal clan which lived on the peninsula and to the west of what is now Albany.

GEOLOGY

The Torndirrup Peninsula is composed of three major rock types. The oldest of these, the gneisses, took their current form amid high pressures and temperatures between 1 300 and 1 600 million years ago, pre-dating almost all life on Earth. One of the best places to see these rocks is at The Gap. Gneisses can be recognised by the 'stripey' pattern within them, caused by layers of different coloured minerals. In many cases, the stripes display bends or folds caused by pressures so high that they made the rocks behave like plasticine. High temperatures and pressures are found at great depths within the Earth's crust.

When the gneisses were formed, Australia was separated from Antarctica. However, over many millions of years, the two continents moved together and collided. At the time of the momentous collision, rocks at the base of the Earth's crust, between the two continents, began to melt and rise slowly. This material then cooled, forming a 'glue' between the continents. The 'glue' can still be seen today – it is the granite of Torndirrup National Park. It is recognised by its large crystals and the characteristic rounded shape of the boulders, known as 'tors'. Granites can also be seen at The Gap, where they are mixed with the much older gneisses in a complex association formed when the rising magma, which hardened into the granite, squeezed into the older rock. The combined continents gradually rose, and the surface eroded until, finally, these rocks were exposed at the surface. The two continents later separated.

WILDFLOWERS AND WILDLIFE

Peppermints grow on the sand hills, and south of Vancouver Peninsula there is a karri forest of medium height with swamp yate. Banksias grow on the northern side of the peninsula's ridge, and the rare Albany woollybush has been found in the park.

The varied vegetation is home to native animals such as pygmy possums, kangaroos, quendas, bush rats and many reptiles. Whales are often seen from the cliffs during winter, and seals sometimes visit the coast.

WHERE IS IT? 10 km south of Albany across Princess Royal Harbour. There is well signposted road access via Frenchman Bay Road. Sealed roads lead to all major features.

TRAVELLING TIME: 15 minutes from Albany.

TOTAL AREA: 3 936 ha.

WHAT TO DO: Walking, whale watching, sightseeing, photography, fishing, rock climbing (for experienced climbers with proper equipment), abseiling. A nearby whaling museum at the old whaling station makes a fascinating visit.

WALKS:

Sharp Point: Easy 500 m, 10 minute circuit to two lookouts to the south and west. Part of the way is suitable for people in assisted wheelchairs.

The Gap/Natural Bridge: Easy 300 m return, 15 minute stroll to spectacular lookouts. Accessible to people in wheelchairs, but a strong fit person will be needed to assist them.

The Blowholes: Medium 1.5 km, 40 minute walk to a crackline in the granite which 'blows' air and occasionally spray.

Jimmy Newhills: Easy 100 m, 6 minute return walk to a lookout over this 'secret' haven.

Stony Hill Heritage Trail: Medium 500 m, 15 minute circuit to lookouts over the highest point in the park with 360° views.

Salmon Holes: Easy 300 m, 10 minute walk to a lookout or steep steps down to the beach.

Bald Head: Hard 10 km return, 6-8 hour bushwalk over Isthmus Hill and Limestone Head, finishing at Bald Head.

FACILITIES: None within the park. However there are barbecues, tables, a shop, toilets and caravan parks nearby. A recreation camp at Quaranup is run by the Ministry of Sport and Recreation. Contact them for more information and bookings.

NEAREST CALM OFFICE: CALM's South Coast Regional Office is at 120 Albany Highway, Albany, phone (08) 9842 4500.

TAKE CARE ON THE COAST: The Torndirrup coastline has a notorious record for accidents and deaths, due to people being washed into the ocean by freak waves, gusting winds or extra large swells. Please exercise extreme caution and don't risk being the next victim.

FACING PAGE
Sharp Point seen from the Natural Bridge area. Photo – Jiri Lochman

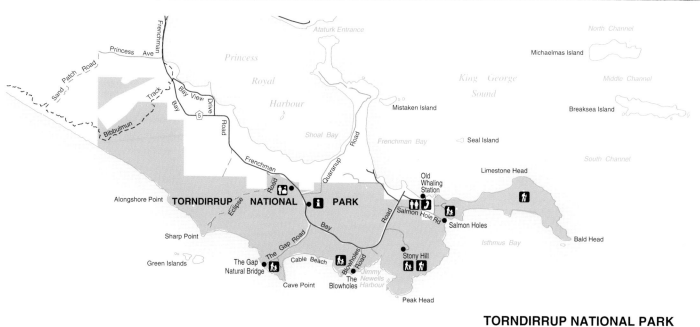

TORNDIRRUP NATIONAL PARK

Scale
0 1 2 3 4 5 km

Porongurup National Park

The granite domes of the Porongurup Range rise over the plain 40 kilometres north of Albany. Twelve kilometres long and 670 metres at its highest point, the Porongurup Range is renowned for its beauty. The Range is clothed in a luxuriant forest of tall karri trees, and the forest understorey puts on a brilliant display of wildflowers during spring and early summer.

As well as the beauty of the moss-covered granite rocks and the lush forest, the views from the Porongurup Range are magnificent. From the peaks and other vantage points, the Stirling Range is clearly visible to the north and, on a clear day, you can see the Southern Ocean to the south.

BUSH RAMBLES

The 'Tree in the Rock' picnic area, set among the karri trees, almost has the feel of a cathedral, with the towering karris providing the domed roof. The tree after which the site has been named is just 100 metres along a shaded walk. Extending its roots down through a crevice, this mature karri clings to existence on a granite boulder.

Many unusual rock formations make the Porongurup Range a fascinating place for picnicking and bush rambles. The Tree in the Rock picnic area is a haven for birds, such as rufous treecreepers, golden whistlers and brilliant scarlet and yellow robins. Footpaths lead to several peaks, other paths cross the range, and a nature trail winds through the forest near the Tree in the Rock.

At the eastern end of the range is Castle Rock. A four kilometre return walk takes you past the famous balancing rock then some rock scrambling and a steep climb allows you to stand on the 'battlements' of Castle Rock. There are great views of the surrounding countryside.

CLOTHED WITH KARRI

The karri (*Eucalyptus diversicolor*) trees that grow on the slopes of the Porongurup Range are a remnant from former times. Karri forest grows exclusively on a deep red soil known as karri loam, and needs at least 700 millimetres of rain each year. Fossil pollen found in many places throughout WA indicates that in an earlier, wetter era karri forest grew far beyond its present extent. As the climate became drier, the forest gradually retreated west to its current stronghold between Manjimup and Walpole. In places where the soil was suitable, and the rainfall remained high enough, small outlying populations survived. Hence, a virtual island of karri forest still survives in the range.

Colonial botanist James Drummond, who visited the range in 1843 and 1848 to collect plant specimens for shipment to other botanists in England, described the karris as 'the finest trees I have ever seen in any country'. The majestic karri is the tallest tree in WA, sometimes reaching 80 metres

high. The trees growing at the Porongurup Range, however, only attain heights of about 40 metres. They are able to survive in the range in sheltered gullies and in places where there is more moisture from run-off.

WHERE IS IT? 40 km north of Albany via Chester Pass Road, the Mount Barker-Porongurup Road and Bolganup Road.

TRAVELLING TIME: 40 minutes from Albany.

TOTAL AREA: 2 621 ha.

WHAT TO DO: Bushwalking, picnicking, rock climbing (for experienced climbers with proper equipment), abseiling.

WALKS:

Bolganup Heritage Trail: Easy 600 m, 30 minute circuit.

The Pass: Easy 2 km, 1 hour return walk.

Devils Slide: Medium 4 km, 2 hour return walk. Not recommended in wet conditions due to slippery rocks.

Marmabup Rock: Hard 5 km, 3 hour return walk via Devils Slide. Recommended only for experienced bushwalkers.

Hayward Peak: Medium 3 km, 2 hour return walk from the Tree in the Rock picnic area to Hayward Peak and back.

Nancy Peak Loop: Strenuous 5.5 km, 2-3 hour circuit from the Tree in the Rock picnic area. The path heads up the northern side of the range and then along its very spine, up and over Hayward Peak, Nancy Peak and Morgans View. Carry plenty of drinking water.

Castle Rock: This medium 4 km, 2 hour walk at the eastern end of the park takes you past the famous balancing rock and up to stand on Castle Rock. The last section of the walk is difficult.

FACILITIES: Free gas barbecues, toilets and picnic tables. Fees apply to enter the park.

NEAREST CALM OFFICE: A resident ranger, based at the main entrance on Bolganup Road, looks after the park. CALM's South Coast Regional Office is at 120 Albany Highway, Albany, phone (08) 9842 4500.

FACING PAGE
Marmabup Peak. Photo – Marie Lochman

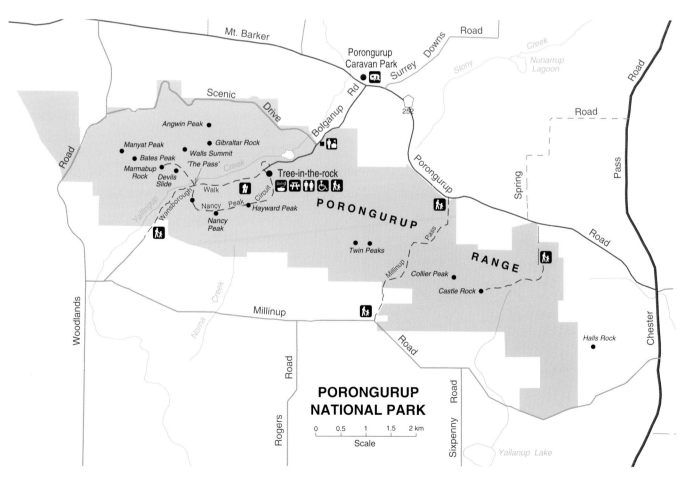

**PORONGURUP
NATIONAL PARK**

0   0.5   1   1.5   2 km
Scale

Stirling Range National Park

The brooding beauty of the mountain landscape, its stunning and unique wildflowers and the challenge of climbing Bluff Knoll have long drawn bushwalkers and climbers to the Stirling Range National Park. Bluff Knoll, at 1 095 metres above sea level, is the highest peak in the South-West. The main face of the Bluff forms one of the most impressive cliffs on the Australian mainland. It takes three to four hours to complete the five kilometre return walk to the summit.

The jagged peaks of the Stirling Range stretch for 65 kilometres from east to west. The rocks of the range were once sands and silts deposited in the delta of a river flowing into a shallow sea. Deposited over many millions of years, these layers of sediment became so thick and heavy that, in combination with unimaginable forces stretching the Earth's crust in the area, they caused the crust to sink. As the surface subsided, still more sediment was deposited in the depression which was left. The final thickness of sediment is believed to be more than 1.6 kilometres! As the sediment built up, so did the pressure on the layers below. The water was forced out of these layers, which solidified to become rocks known as sandstones and shales.

Buried deep in the Earth's crust, the rocks which form today's Stirling Range were gradually exposed over millions of years as the surrounding rocks were worn away by the forces of weathering (chemical breakdown) and erosion (physical removal of material by water, wind and gravity). It was during this process that the current form of the range was sculptured.

HISTORY

The Qaaniyan and Koreng Aboriginal people originally lived around the range. In cold weather they wore kangaroo skin cloaks reaching nearly to the knee. They also established small, conical huts in wet weather. Sticks were placed in the ground and bent to form a cone, then threaded with paperbark, rushes or leafy branches. They told many stories about the Stirling Range, and in many of them the range is hostile and dangerous.

Bluff Knoll was called Pualaar Miial (great many-faced hill) by the local Aboriginal people, because the rocks on the Bluff were shaped like faces. The peak is often covered with mists, which curl around the mountain tops and float into the gullies. These constantly changing mists were believed to be the only visible form of a spirit called Noatch (meaning dead body or corpse), who had an evil reputation.

The range was first recorded by Matthew Flinders in 1802. In 1831 Surgeon Alexander Collie recorded the Aboriginal name of the range, 'Koi Kyeunu-ruff', which was provided to him by his Aboriginal guide Mokare. Surveyor-General John Septimus Roe travelled to Perth with Governor Sir James Stirling in 1835, and glimpsed 'some remarkable and elevated peaks'. Roe called them the Stirling Range. The area was declared a national park in 1913, at a time when the dominant culture was towards clearing the bush and converting it to farmland.

WILDFLOWER WONDERLAND

The number and beauty of the wildflowers is staggering. The park is one of the world's most important areas for flora, with 1 500 species (many of which grow nowhere else) packed within its boundaries. More plant species occur in the Stirling Range than in the entire British Isles, and 82 plant species found in the Stirling Range occur nowhere else on Earth. This tally includes the famous mountain bells of the genus *Darwinia*. Needless to say, spring wildflower viewing is incredible.

Because of their height, and proximity to the South Coast, the climate on the peaks differs from that of surrounding areas. This is the main reason for the great variety of wildflowers. There are, for instance, an astonishing 123 orchid species – 38 per cent of all known Western Australian orchids. Between August and December, the white flowers of southern cross (*Xanthosia rotundifolia*), which resemble the four stars of the Southern Cross constellation, are a common sight.

*Southern cross (*Xanthosia rotundifolia*). Photo – Babs & Bert Wells/CALM*

FACING PAGE
Bluff Knoll. Photo – Gordon Roberts

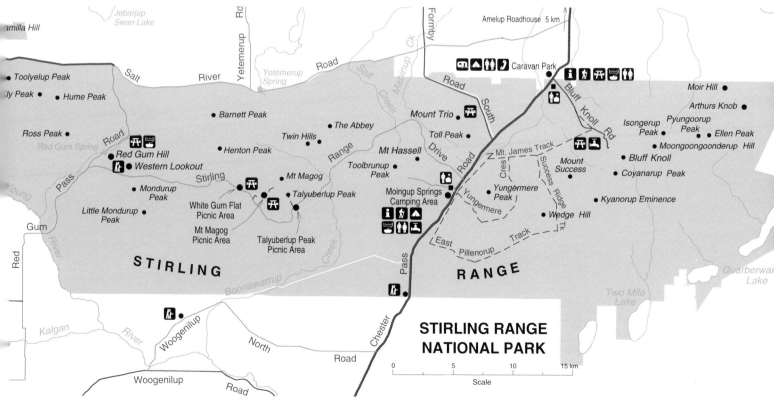

**STIRLING RANGE
NATIONAL PARK**

Scale

0   5   10   15 km

Thicket grows on the upper levels of all the major peaks. In spring, the thicket is a mass of flowering shrubs. The brilliant pink of Stirling Range pixie mop (*Isopogon latifolius*) contrasts strongly with the reds of the *Nemcia* species, the yellow of *Dryandra* and the white of the giant candles (*Andersonia axilliflora*). This mass flowering arrives later than that on the lowlands, and can be seen to best advantage in October, especially on a misty day when the clouds around the mountains enclose the visitor into this world of colour without the vista of the surrounding farmland.

CLIMATE, CLOUDS AND SNOW

An ideal time to visit is in late spring and early summer (October to December), when days are beginning to warm up and the wildflowers are at their best. Winter, between June and August, is cold and wet, and visitors should come prepared. Even in spring the weather can be unpredictable, particularly higher up in the range. Sudden cold changes cause the temperature to drop, and rain or hail to set in. All visitors are strongly advised not to enter the bush or use footpaths on days of extreme fire danger.

The Stirling Range is renowned for its unusual, and sometimes spectacular, cloud formations. Park visitors may notice two types of unusual cloud formations about the peaks, often when the rest of the sky is clear. A shallow, low-level stratified cloud that drapes over the higher peaks is a familiar sight. Another type of shallow cloud layer may leave the higher peaks exposed, which is a unique sight in WA.

The range is one of few places in WA where snow occasionally falls. Snow probably falls on the highest peaks several times each year. On most occasions, it is only a light dusting or the snow melts on impact. However, falls above five centimetres have been reported on Bluff Knoll. Snow may occur at any time in winter and sometimes in spring.

Catspaws. Photo – Gordon Roberts/CALM

View of Stirling Range with banksias in foreground. Photo – Gordon Roberts/CALM

Above: View of Mt Magog, Talyuberlup Peak and Toolbrunup Peak. Photo – Cliff Winfield

Below: Common mountain bell (Darwinia lejostyla). Photo – Babs & Bert Wells/CALM

WHERE IS IT? The park is about 100 km north-east of Albany via Chester Pass Road.

TRAVELLING TIME: Just over 1 hour from Albany.

TOTAL AREA: 115 920 ha.

WHAT TO DO: Bushwalking, mountain climbing, camping, picnicking, birdwatching, wildflower viewing.

WALKS:

Bluff Knoll: This 5 km return, 3-4 hour walk is of medium difficulty, if taken slowly.

Toolbrunup: Hard 4 km, 3-4 hour walk with magnificent 360° views from the summit. (Rock scramble for the last third of the walk).

Mount Magog: Hard (no path for final 1 km to the summit) 8 km, 3-4 hour return walk.

Talyuberlup: Medium 3 km, 2-3 hour return walk.

Mount Hassell: Medium 4 km, 2-3 hour return walk.

Mount Trio: Medium 3 km, 2 hour return walk.

WARNING: Walking is not recommended in wet or windy conditions or in extreme heat.

FACILITIES: Gas barbecues, toilets and picnic tables. There is a camping area at Moingup Springs.

NEAREST CALM OFFICE: There are two resident rangers, one at the turn-off to Bluff Knoll and the other at Park Headquarters, near Moingup Springs in Chester Pass. CALM's South Coast Regional Office is at 120 Albany Highway, Albany, phone (08) 9842 4500.

Two Peoples Bay Reserve

Two Peoples Bay is one of Australia's most important reserves, and it has been proposed as a national park. It is the home of the vulnerable noisy scrub-bird and the only place where the critically endangered Gilbert's potoroo (a small relation of kangaroos and wallabies), previously thought to be extinct, is known to exist. Other rare species include the western bristlebird and western whipbird.

As well as some stunning coastline, the reserve protects an area of dense heath, low forest and swampland typical of this part of the South Coast, with occasional deeper gullies which support the thick scrub favoured by the noisy scrub-bird.

NOISY SCRUB-BIRD

The noisy scrub-bird, a near-flightless bird with an ear-rattling call, was first sighted in jarrah forest of the Darling Range near Perth in 1842, and the last recorded specimen had been collected at Torbay in 1889. The bird was not seen or heard again for 72 years, and many ornithologists considered it to be extinct. However, it was rediscovered here in December 1961, in an area that had been proposed as a new townsite. After the bird's rediscovery, the State government set the area aside as a nature reserve.

Since 1983, noisy scrub-birds from Two Peoples Bay have been released in several places east and west of Albany. When released into good habitat that is protected from fire, the birds will breed and their offspring gradually colonise all of the available habitat. In this way, the total number of noisy scrub-birds has increased tenfold since the species was rediscovered, and the population is now spread along almost 50 kilometres of the coast around Two Peoples Bay. The bird has also been reintroduced into some of its former territory in the Darling Range near Harvey, 150 years after it was first discovered there.

GILBERT'S POTOROO

An exciting and unexpected spin-off from the conservation of the noisy scrub-bird came late in 1994, when a small, rabbit-sized marsupial called Gilbert's potoroo (*Potorous gilbertii*) was found on the slopes of Mount Gardner. This animal had not been reliably reported anywhere in the South-West for more than 100 years, and had been officially proclaimed extinct.

Potoroos specialise in eating underground fungi, and this nocturnal and appealing little animal had been quietly going about its truffle-hunting business beneath the Mount Gardner scrub, unseen for many years. But it must have come very close to extinction. Despite intensive efforts, only 15 individuals were recorded in the first year after rediscovery. The search is continuing.

Below: Noisy scrub-bird.
Below right: Gilbert's potoroo. Photos – Jiri Lochman

OTHER BIRDS AND MAMMALS

The Two Peoples Bay Reserve is unusually rich in birds, with 188 recorded species. Some of these are seabirds, like the great-winged petrels, flesh-footed shearwaters and little penguins, which breed on Coffin Island. Others are transequatorial waders or nomadic species of honeyeaters, lorikeets and pardalotes, which appear in response to seasonal blossom. The majority, however, are residents that breed within the reserve.

Like the noisy scrub-bird, some also face problems of low numbers and reduced ranges. The western bristlebird is found in the dense heaths on the sandy slopes of Mount Gardner, and is currently designated as an endangered species. So is the western whipbird, an inhabitant of the scrubby thickets. Both birds had ranged as far north as the Perth area, where they were recorded last century. By the middle of this century, their ranges had contracted to only a few places including the Two Peoples Bay area, and their numbers around the time the nature reserve was created were very low.

The park is also a haven for other rare and uncommon mammals. The diggings of the quenda are common. At times, areas particularly favoured by these omnivorous bandicoots resemble newly dug-over vegetable gardens. Quendas are often seen during the day, crossing roads and tracks within the reserve, and are taken by birds of prey such as the little eagle. Ringtail possums are occasionally seen in the low forest trees on Mount Gardner, where their dreys (basketball-sized nests made of sticks) are common.

For many years, the population of quokkas on Mount Gardner was one of few known on the mainland. These small mammals make tunnel-like runs through thick vegetation. Seldom seen in the thick cover, the runs and their distinctive droppings are often the only sign of their presence.

You can learn more about the rare wildlife, and the success of the reintroduction work at the Two Peoples Bay Visitor Centre.

The reserve is closed on the days when the fire danger is extreme. Signs will notify visitors of any closures.

Above: Mt Manypeaks viewed from the Baie des deux Peuples Heritage Trail.
Photo – Marie Lochman

WHERE IS IT? 35 km east of Albany via Lower King Road and Two Peoples Bay Road.

TRAVELLING TIME: 30 minutes from Albany.

TOTAL AREA: 4 744 ha.

WHAT TO DO: Picnicking, bushwalking, birdwatching, fishing, snorkelling, scuba diving.

WALKS:

Baie des deux Peuples Heritage Trail: Medium 2 km, 1 hour circuit that explores the history and flora of Two Peoples Bay.

Visitor Centre to Little Beach: Easy 5 km, 3 hour return walk.

FACILITIES: Visitor centre, gas barbecues, toilets.

NEAREST CALM OFFICE: The reserve is managed by a resident ranger. Other CALM staff work at the reserve on research programs. CALM's South Coast Regional Office is at 120 Albany Highway, Albany, phone (08) 9842 4500.

Above: View of Mt Gardner headland from the north end of Two Peoples Bay.
Photo – Dennis Sarson/Lochman Transparencies

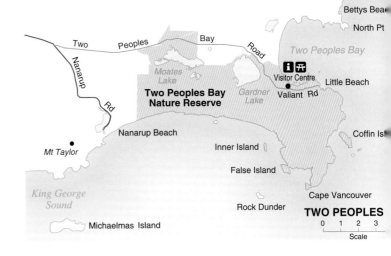

Bettys Beach
North Pt
Two Peoples Bay
Two   Peoples   Bay   Road
Nanarup
Moates Lake
Visitor Centre
Little Beach
Two Peoples Bay Nature Reserve
Gardner Lake
Valiant Rd
Rd
Coffin Is
Nanarup Beach
Inner Island
Mt Taylor
False Island
Cape Vancouver
King George Sound
Rock Dunder
TWO PEOPLES
0   1   2   3
Scale
Michaelmas Island

Waychinicup National Park

Waychinicup National Park extends from Normans Beach, across Mount Manypeaks and the Waychinicup River mouth, to Cheyne Beach, not far from Albany. The area is very scenic, with unusual granite rock formations and views both inland and along the coast. The protected inlet of the Waychinicup River is most popular for fishing and swimming, and is extremely picturesque, with polished granite rocks tumbled along both sides.

The coastal heath around Waychinicup is exceptionally diverse and in spring it is awash with colourful wildflowers. Waychinicup is derived from the Nyoongar word 'waitch', which means 'emu', and 'up', which means 'place of'. The name first appeared on maps in 1877.

Access to Waychinicup National Park is via a rough gravel road accessible to two-wheel-drive vehicles.

WHERE IS IT? The park is about 65 km east of Albany via the South Coast Highway and Cheyne Beach Road, with a spur road taking visitors to the Waychinicup Inlet.

TRAVELLING TIME: 1 hour.

TOTAL AREA: 6 310 ha.

WHAT TO DO: Bushwalking, rock climbing (for experienced climbers with proper equipment), fishing.

FACILITIES: Bush camping is permitted (camping fees apply), but space is limited and the only facilities are gas barbecues and toilets. No fires are permitted. Accommodation is available at nearby Cheyne Beach Caravan Park, which is just outside the park boundary.

NEAREST CALM OFFICE: CALM's South Coast Regional Office is at 120 Albany Highway, Albany, phone (08) 9842 4500.

Waychinicup River. Photo – Gordon Roberts

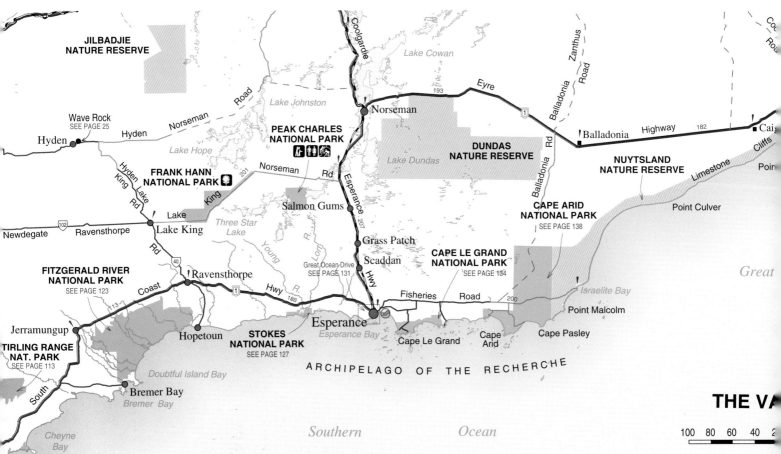

JILBADJIE NATURE RESERVE

Wave Rock
SEE PAGE 25

Hyden

Hyden

Norseman Road

Lake Johnston

Coolgardie

Lake Cowan

Zanthus

Balladonia Road

Co...
Roa...

PEAK CHARLES NATIONAL PARK

Norseman

193

Eyre

1

Balladonia

Highway

182

Cai...

Cliffs

DUNDAS NATURE RESERVE

Lake Dundas

Balladonia Rd

NUYTSLAND NATURE RESERVE

Limestone

Poin...

Lake Hope

FRANK HANN NATIONAL PARK

Norseman   Rd

201

King

Hyden Lake King Rd

Salmon Gums

Esperance 207

CAPE ARID NATIONAL PARK
SEE PAGE 138

Point Culver

Newdegate

102

Ravensthorpe

Lake King

Lake

Rd

Three Star Lake

Young R.

Lord R.

Great Ocean Drive
SEE PAGE 131

Grass Patch

Scaddan

CAPE LE GRAND NATIONAL PARK
SEE PAGE 134

Great

FITZGERALD RIVER NATIONAL PARK
SEE PAGE 123

40

Ravensthorpe

1

Hwy   188

Coast

113

Hwy

Esperance

Fisheries   Road

200

Israelite Bay

Point Malcolm

Jerramungup

TIRLING RANGE NAT. PARK
SEE PAGE 113

South

Hopetoun

STOKES NATIONAL PARK
SEE PAGE 127

Esperance Bay

Cape Le Grand

Cape Arid

Cape Pasley

Doubtful Island Bay

ARCHIPELAGO OF THE RECHERCHE

THE VA

Bremer Bay

Bremer Bay

Cheyne Bay

Southern   Ocean

100 80 60 40 2

The Vast South-East

Bremer Bay to Eucla

Once east of Albany, you are on the edge of the vast south-east. Distances are greater, towns fewer, and the national parks and reserves are much more remote. Much of the farmland was only cleared in the 1950s or later, and the reserves here often protect pristine natural environments.

The fragile vegetation communities of WA's southern coast contain an enormous variety of flowering plants, many of which are locally endemic, that is, they only grow wild in very small areas of this long coast. National parks, such as Fitzgerald River, contain a greater variety of plants in only a few thousand hectares than occurs across entire countries in some other parts of the world. This range of species gives rise to some fascinating adaptations. Banksias have been identified with Australia since Joseph Banks collected the first specimens from the east coast in the eighteenth century. The coastal vegetation communities between Albany and Israelite Bay are largely dominated by banksias and other members of the Proteaceae family. Because Proteaceae are highly susceptible to dieback (the fungus *Phytophthora cinnamomi*), these areas are very prone to infection.

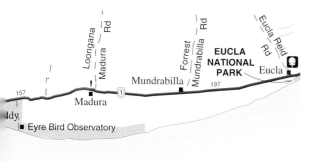

FACING PAGE
Spongelite cliffs, Twertup. Photo – Dennis Sarson/Lochman Transparencies
Honey possum on Baxter's banksia (Banksia baxteri). Photo – Babs and Bert Wells/CALM

OUTH-EAST

ale

Fitzgerald River National Park

Surrounding the inlets of the Gairdner, Fitzgerald and Hamersley Rivers, between Bremer Bay and Hopetoun on the southern coast of WA, lies one of the last great wilderness areas of the south. This extraordinary area is the only national park in WA to be gazetted as a World Biosphere Reserve. While some areas within the natural park can be reached by conventional vehicle, others are only accessible by four-wheel-drive, and in much of the central core access is only by foot.

WILDFLOWERS

Fitzgerald River National Park contains a range of plants that are as startling as they are delicate. It is famed as one of the most diverse botanical regions in the world. More than 1 700 beautiful and bizarre plant species, as well as a myriad of lichens, mosses and fungi, have been found in the park. This is nearly 20 per cent of the total number of plant species in WA, found in an area that covers only 0.1 per cent of the State. More than 70 of these are endemic to the park, and dozens more are almost confined to the park. Foremost among them is the royal hakea (*Hakea victoria*), with its brightly coloured, variegated leaves. When sunlit from above or behind, the leaves appear to glow like lanterns.

A short walk to the base of East Mount Barren will reveal the silver-leaved Barrens regelia (*Regelia velutina*), the red-flowering Barrens clawflower (*Calothamnus validus*) and the veined jugflower (*Adenanthos venosus*). A pea-flowering jacksonia (*Jacksonia compressa*) has dispensed with leaves; a flattened stem serves the same purpose. Another distinctive plant here is the miniature pine look-alike, dense clawflower (*Calothamnus pinifolius*). If the plant is flowering, it is easy to see where the common name came from.

Oak leaf dryandra (*Dryandra quercifolia*) is restricted to the park and its immediate vicinity, but it grows on many soil types. Mountain banksia (*Banksia oreophila*) is so named as it occurs only on the Barrens, the Stirling Range and a few coastal mountains. The graceful weeping gum (*Eucalyptus sepulcralis*) grows only on quartzite in the park. It was given the name *sepulcralis*, which means 'of the tomb', as this forlorn-looking species was thought to be ideal for cemeteries.

GEOLOGY

The area has a rugged beauty with small but spectacular quartzite mountains, mostly near the coast. The park is also famous for its white spongelite cliffs, which are exposed along the Fitzgerald and Hamersley rivers. Silica skeletons of sponges, deposited here some 43 million years ago when a warm sea invaded the landscape, are a major component of this rock, which is known as spongelite.

At this time, the sea level was considerably higher than its present level, and the 'Barrens' were then islands. Fifty metres above the present coastline, ocean waves cut a platform into the uplands and around the once partially submerged Barren Ranges, and these can still be seen today, now marooned high and dry. As the sea level fell again, the rivers draining the hinterlands cut deeply into the soft spongelite of the marine plain, forming gorges between 10 and 50 metres deep in the colourful rock.

VISITING THE FITZGERALD

Before you visit the park, it is advisable to contact the rangers to find out about local weather conditions and road closures. Camping areas are provided, both in the western and eastern ends of the park. At St Marys (close to Point Ann), accessible by two-wheel-drive from the western end, there are 14 individual campsites, day-use shelters, ablutions and free gas barbecues. Whale watching from a purpose-built platform at Point Ann is popular from June to the end of October. Southern right whales can be seen cavorting before the spectacular backdrop of Thumb Peak on most days during the whale season. Other activities include fishing, walking the Point Ann Heritage Trail, beachcombing and swimming. Depending on weather conditions, the Fitzgerald Inlet bush camping site further east can be accessed by four-wheel-drive.

At the eastern end of the park is Four Mile Beach camping area. This can be reached by two-wheel-drive and is a convenient place to camp when visiting East Mount Barren, Barrens Beach, Mylies Beach and West Beach.

Quoin Head can be reached by four-wheel-drive, and is a wonderful place to experience some of the most rugged coast the Fitzgerald has to offer. Ospreys are seen regularly, often sparring in the air with kestrels and Australian hobbies. Facilities here are basic, with a small number of marked camping bays, gas barbecues and toilets.

The park may be closed to vehicles during wet weather. Please ask at the ranger station, or at CALM's Albany office, for updates on conditions.

Royal hakea (Hakea victoria). *Photo – Babs & Bert Wells/CALM*

FACING PAGE
Point Ann whale lookout, Fitzgerald River National Park.
Photo – Bill Belson/Lochman Transparencies

WHERE IS IT? 30 km south-east of Esperance, 50 km by road. Approach via Fisheries Road, Merivale Road and Cape Le Grand Road. The route is well signposted from Fisheries Road. Visitor fees apply.

TRAVELLING TIME: 30 minutes from Esperance.

TOTAL AREA: 32 100 ha.

WHAT TO DO: Walking, camping (fees apply), snorkelling, picnicking, swimming, fishing.

WALKS:

Coastal Trail: 15 km one-way, allow 6-8 hours. May be broken into four shorter sections:

- **Le Grand Beach to Hellfire Bay:** Hard 2-3 hour walk.
- **Hellfire Bay to Thistle Cove:** Hard 2 hour walk.
- **Thistle Cove to Lucky Bay:** Easy 30 minute walk.
- **Lucky Bay to Rossiter Bay:** Medium 2-3 hour walk.

Frenchman Peak: Hard 3 km return, 2 hour walk. Please follow the footpath from the car park to the easy angled east slope – do not attempt to short cut as the rock is deceptively steep, especially on descent. Not recommended in wet or windy weather.

Le Grand Heritage Trail: Easy 1.5 km, 40 minute circuit from Thistle Cove car park along the Coastal Trail to Lucky Bay.

Bird Sanctuary: Easy 400 m, 15 minute return stroll from Rossiter Bay car park.

FACILITIES: Gas barbecues, toilets, picnic areas, shade shelters, water. There are campsites (with septic toilets and showers) at Lucky Bay and Le Grand Beach.

NEAREST CALM OFFICE: The park has a resident ranger near the main entrance on Cape Le Grand Road and a mobile ranger based at Lucky Bay during summer. CALM's Esperance District Office is at 92 Dempster Street, Esperance, phone (08) 9071 3733.

Above: Frenchman Peak.

Below: Picnickers at Thistle Cove. Photos – Jiri Lochman

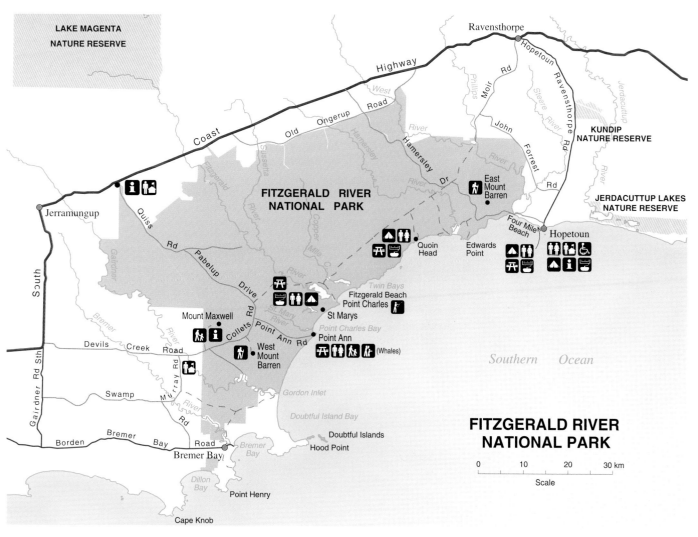

LAKE MAGENTA
NATURE RESERVE

Ravensthorpe

Highway

West

Road

Old   Ongerup   Road

Coast

Jerramungup

KUNDIP
NATURE RESERVE

JERDACUTTUP LAKES
NATURE RESERVE

FITZGERALD RIVER
NATIONAL PARK

East
Mount Barren

Hopetoun

Quoin Head

Edwards
Point

Four Mile
Beach

South

Twin Bays

Fitzgerald Beach
Point Charles

St Marys

Mount Maxwell

Point Charles Bay

Point Ann

Devils   Creek   Road

West
Mount
Barren

(Whales)

Southern   Ocean

Swamp

Gordon Inlet

Doubtful Island Bay

Borden   Bremer   Bay   Road

Doubtful Islands

Hood Point

Bremer Bay

Bremer
Bay

**FITZGERALD RIVER
NATIONAL PARK**

Dillon
Bay

0   10   20   30 km

Scale

Point Henry

Cape Knob

WHERE IS IT? The park is about 180 km north-east of Albany via South Coast Highway and Devils Creek Road. It is a similar distance from Esperance via the South Coast Highway and the Ravensthorpe-Hopetoun Road. Entry fees apply.

TRAVELLING TIME: 2 hours from Albany or Esperance. However, travel within this large park can be slow.

TOTAL AREA: 329 039 ha.

WHAT TO DO: Camping (fees apply), bushwalking (please notify park rangers when going on extended walks), fishing, four-wheel-driving, whale watching.

WALKS:

Mount Maxwell: Easy 100 m, 5 minute stroll to a lookout.

West Mount Barren: Medium 3 km, 2 hour return walk follows a marked path to the summit.

Point Ann Heritage Trail: Easy 1.5 km, 60 minute circuit with magnificent coastal views and potential whale sightings in winter and spring.

East Mount Barren: Hard 4 km return, 3 hour walk. A steep path ascends the south-western spur of the peak. Not recommended in wet or windy weather. Interpretive brochure available on site.

FACILITIES: Field studies centre (Twertup).

Point Ann - Picnic shelters, whale watching platform, toilets, heritage trail with boot cleaning station at start of walk.
St Marys - Gas barbecues, tent sites, toilets, tables.
Quoin Head - Gas barbecues, tent sites, toilets, tables.
Fitzgerald Inlet - Gas barbecues, tent sites, toilets, tables.
Four Mile Beach - Gas barbeques, tent sites, toilets, tables.

NEAREST CALM OFFICE: Rangers are stationed in the park. Park headquarters are a short distance along Quiss Rd from the South Coast Highway, phone (08) 9835 5043. CALM's South Coast Regional Office is at 120 Albany Highway, Albany, phone (08) 9842 4500.

Top left: View of Thumb Peak. Photo – Jiri Lochman
Left: Southern right whale. Photo – Dorothy Bail

Frank Hann National Park

A tourist, deeply impressed by the display of floral colour as he drove from Norseman to Lake King in 1969, petitioned the government of the day to preserve the area. The government responded by making it a national park. The park was named after surveyor and explorer Frank Hann, who traversed the area in 1901.

There are no facilities or developed visitor sites in this park, but people can still enjoy the drive through it along the Lake King-Norseman Road. Spring and early summer (September through to January) is the best time for a visit, but something is in flower all year round.

FULL OF FLOWERS

On the deeper sandy soil mallees are the dominant plants, forming an open upper canopy over several layers of shrubs and annuals such as everlastings during good seasons. Snap and rattle (*Eucalyptus gracilis*), tall sand mallee (*Eucalyptus eremophila*), capped mallee (*Eucalyptus pileata*), Fremantle mallee (*Eucalyptus foecunda*) and the mallee form of red morrell (*Eucalyptus longicornis*) are common.

Four different banksia species can be recognised in shrubby areas. Swordfish banksia (*Banksia elderiana*) is a large, scruffy shrub whose golden flowers, produced in summer, hang downwards from the branches. Another golden-flowered banksia, flowering a little earlier, is cannonball banksia (*Banksia lemanniana*). It is a sparser, upright bush, with solid, spherical fruits. Southern plains banksia (*Banksia media*) forms a large, rounded shrub with prominent yellow flower-spikes in autumn through to winter. Violet banksia (*Banksia violacea*) is much smaller, with needle-shaped leaves and small violet flowers in early summer.

Wattles, sheoaks and melaleucas, such as broom bush (*Melaleuca uncinata*), tend to be the dominant plants in areas of thicket, with diverse but sparse layers of shorter shrubs beneath them. The ground layer often includes everlastings and orchids.

Featherflowers are a colourful part of the heathland vegetation. A yellow featherflower (*Verticordia chrysantha*), the painted featherflower (*Verticordia picta*) which is pink, the rapier featherflower (*Verticordia mitchelliana*) which is red, and the extraordinary bush cauliflower (*Verticordia eriocephala*) – whose small, crowded white flower heads look, from a distance, exactly like that vegetable – are among those found in the park.

Pincushions (Borya species) in summer. Photo – Jiri Lochman

WHERE IS IT? 40 km east of Lake King and 90 km north of Ravensthorpe.

TRAVELLING TIME: 40 minutes from Lake King, 1½ hours from Ravensthorpe.

TOTAL AREA: 67 550 ha.

WHAT TO DO: Scenic driving.

FACILITIES: There are no facilities in this remote area and no supplies between Lake King and Norseman, so visitors must be self-sufficient.

NEAREST CALM OFFICE: CALM's Esperance District Office is at 92 Dempster Street, Esperance, phone (08) 9071 3733.

Stokes National Park

Stokes Inlet, in Stokes National Park, is one of the most picturesque and interesting estuaries along WA's southern coast. The inlet covers around 14 square kilometres, and features long beaches and rocky headlands backed by sand dunes and low hills. Dense bush and shady paperbark trees grow right to the beaches along the water's edge.

Stokes Inlet is the largest of a number of estuaries around Esperance, and is the only one with reasonably deep water. The Young and the Lort Rivers flow into the upper reaches of the inlet but, when the water level is low in summer, they are cut off from the lagoon by a wide river delta. The mouth of the estuary lies in the middle of Dunster Castle Bay. This too is cut off from the sea by a high sand bar. This only breaks every few years, and then only for a few weeks. As a result, the salinity and water level of the estuary varies greatly with river flow and evaporation.

A short distance from the shores of Stokes Inlet lie the ruins of the Moir Homestead, consisting of roofless limestone walls. In 1873, Alexander and John Moir were granted a lease of 14 000 acres around Stokes Inlet, extended by 57 000 acres in 1888. The Moirs established a homestead near the eastern shore of the inlet and grazed sheep through the coastal vegetation, which they burned in patterns to provide fresh feed. They shipped their wool from nearby Fanny Cove, together with valuable sandalwood they gathered from the surrounding country. In the 1890s, the cove was used by miners going to the Dundas and Norseman goldfields. A small area was cleared near the homestead and barley and other grain crops were grown as feed for the stock.

WILDFLOWERS AND WILDLIFE

The national park protects Stokes Inlet and the surrounding heathland and lake systems. Yate, swamp yate and paperbarks form dense, low

forests near the wetlands. In autumn, look for the magnificent yellow flowers of the bell-fruited mallee, which only grows about a metre high. Keep an eye open for tiger snakes when walking.

At least 29 species of waterbird have been observed at Stokes Inlet, including large numbers of Australian shelduck, grey teal, little black cormorants, black swans and chestnut teal. Migratory species include the common sandpiper. Red-capped plovers, Australasian grebes, Australian pelicans, little pied cormorants, white-faced herons, great egrets and pied oystercatchers also live in the inlet.

RECREATION

The park is a great place for birdwatchers, because of the impressive abundance of wildlife that frequents the inlet, its shores and associated lakes. The inlet is also popular for fishing and canoeing, and it is possible to launch small boats from the campsites. Be aware, however, that although the area of water looks large there are extensive areas of shallows and rocks. Normal fisheries regulations apply in national parks. Species caught include black bream, Australian salmon, King George whiting and mullet.

There are two campsites on the shores of the inlet. Simple bush toilets are provided. Stokes Inlet itself is the most visited site, but Fanny Cove and Shoal Cape offer attractive coastal scenery accessible only by four-wheel-drive. A one kilometre heritage trail provides excellent views over Stokes Inlet and is interpreted by plaques along the way.

WHERE IS IT? 80 km west of Esperance via the South Coast Highway and Stokes Inlet Road. Entry fees apply.

TRAVELLING TIME: 1 hour from Esperance.

TOTAL AREA: 9 726 ha.

WHAT TO DO: Camping (fees apply), fishing, canoeing, walking, birdwatching, four-wheel-driving.

WALKS:

Stokes Heritage Trail: Easy 2 km, 45 minute circuit.

FACILITIES: Barbecues, bush toilets, picnic tables.

NEAREST CALM OFFICE: CALM's Esperance District Office is at 92 Dempster Street, Esperance, phone (08) 9071 3733. A ranger is stationed in the park.

Ruins of the shepherd's hut on the Moir family property.

FACING PAGE
Saltwater paperbarks fringing Stokes Inlet. Photos – Gordon Roberts/CALM

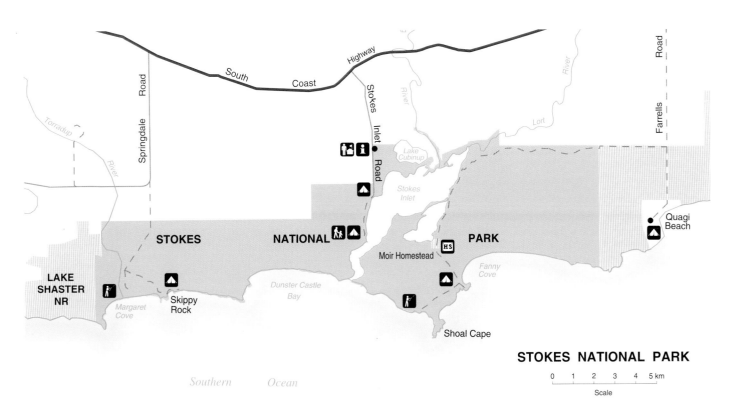

STOKES NATIONAL PARK

0 1 2 3 4 5 km

Scale

Peak Charles National Park

Peak Charles, an ancient granite peak, and its companion, Peak Eleanora, give sweeping views over the dry sandplain heaths and salt lake systems of the surrounding countryside. Towering 500 metres above the surrounding plain, Peak Charles is visible for more than 50 kilometres in all directions.

The granite peaks have weathered to various orange and brown hues. There are many unusual rock formations, and on the slopes of the peaks and in other granite areas many different species of orchid can be found. About 40 million years ago, both peaks were islands, and wave-cut platforms can be seen on their slopes.

A close look at the apparently bare rock reveals many species of lichen and alga, which give a black, grey, green or even orange colour to the surface. The acids they produce help to decompose the rock. At Peak Charles, there are several well-developed 'wave rock' features, where the granite has eroded into the shape of a breaking wave, accentuated by streaks of black algae. It is possible that the algae may be partly responsible for this wave shape.

WILDFLOWERS AND WILDLIFE

Where a depression allows soil and litter to accumulate, a moss sward develops. Soil and water also collect in the fissures, and shrubs may grow there, their roots helping to prise the rock apart.

The combination of water and flowering plants brings numerous birds to these granite islands. Perhaps the most obvious are the birds of prey,

using lift from the rock to spiral upwards and gain height. The thickets, woodlands and flowering scrub surrounding Peak Charles provide habitat for more than 40 different small birds.

WHERE IS IT? 100 km south-west of Norseman via the Coolgardie-Esperance Highway, Lake King-Norseman Road and Peak Charles Road.

TRAVELLING TIME: 2 hours from Norseman, 2½ hours from Esperance.

TOTAL AREA: 39 959 ha.

WHAT TO DO: Camping, bushwalking, rock climbing (for experienced climbers with proper equipment).

WALKS:

Peak Charles Lookout: Medium 2 km, 1 hour climb takes you to the lookout. Beyond the lookout there is no easy way up the final rock slopes to the summit and no route is recommended. All routes require some rock scrambling and steady footing on steeply angled slabs.

FACILITIES: Peak Charles has an area designated for camping, but simple bush toilets are the only facilities. For most of the year there is no fresh water, so if you intend to visit, make sure you are totally self-sufficient. The nearest supplies are at Salmon Gums.

NEAREST CALM OFFICE: CALM's Esperance District Office is at 92 Dempster Street, Esperance, phone (08) 9071 3733.

View of salt lake as seen from Peak Charles. Photo – Jiri Lochman

Esperance

The seaside town of Esperance abounds with opportunities for recreation and scenic attractions. Its bays are sprinkled with more than 100 islands and the white sandy beaches are reputed to be among the best in Australia, if not the world.

HISTORY

The Aboriginal name for the area is Gabba-Kyle, which can be translated as 'the place where the water lies down like a boomerang'. Esperance's European history began in 1627 when the Dutch vessel *Gulden Zeepard* passed through the Archipelago, but did not land in the area. In 1792, two French vessels *L'Esperance* and *L'Recherche* were forced to seek shelter on the Esperance coast from a storm. The first foreign inhabitants of these shores, during the nineteenth century, were sealers from the penal settlement at Van Diemens Land and American and French whalers.

In 1863, the Dempster brothers drove sheep, cattle and horses from Northam to Esperance to take up the first land holding. Andrew Dempster was granted a lease of 100 000 acres in 1895. With the discovery of gold in Dundas, Coolgardie and Kalgoorlie, fortune seekers from Australia and around the world began to flood into this sleepy little port on their way to the Goldfields. By 1897, there were two newspapers, one brewery and four hotels.

However, the town soon dwindled and fell into the doldrums, until Esperance finally emerged in the 1960s as a viable agricultural region. Today, agriculture is still the leading industry but tourism, fishing and other industries are fast developing.

ATTRACTIONS

The Great Ocean Drive is almost obligatory for visitors. It takes in Rotary Lookout on Wireless Hill, wind farms that help to generate electricity for the town and the spectacular swimming beach at Twilight Cove. Observatory Point, where the French vessels sheltered in 1792, has a lookout that also offers great views of the bay and islands.

Pink Lake, which lies just five kilometres west of Esperance, is a major attraction. Algae in the lake provides its unusual colour, which is evident for part of the year. A little further afield, about 12 kilometres west of Esperance, is Monjingup Lake. It provides an insight into an ancient landscape. Some of the zamia palms found at Monjingup Lake are thought to be more than 1 000 years old. The main attraction of the reserve is the small wetland, on which at least 62 different bird species have been observed. A boardwalk, which meanders through paperbark trees, and a bird hide provide excellent opportunities to discover and experience the wonders of this wetland. Barbecues, picnic facilities and an environmental centre enhance the bushland and lakeside setting. The Shire-managed reserve is excellent for birdwatching and wildflowers in spring.

At Helm's Arboretum, 18 kilometres north of Esperance on the Coolgardie-Esperance Highway, you can wander through a large number of native flowering shrubs and trees, along with pines from various countries. Picnic sites and an information bay are provided for visitors. Guided walks at the arboretum are conducted by the Wildflower Society from September to November.

Historic attractions in Esperance include the Dempster Homestead, built in 1897, which can be viewed from the road, and Tommy Windich's grave, the burial place of the faithful friend and companion of early explorer John Forrest. The Museum Village includes a fascinating collection of historic buildings, which house craft shops, a blacksmith, an art gallery, cafe and the Esperance Tourist Bureau.

RECREATION

Awesome, but gentle, southern right whales visit the bays and sheltered inlets, between July and November, to calve. They can be viewed from vantage points on land or by boat. The coastal waters and islands provide a drawcard for boating. Divers can experience crystal clear waters, diverse underwater life, cathedral-like caves, reefs and shipwrecks. The region is an angler's paradise, with snapper, salmon, herring and other popular species readily caught from beaches, jetties or boats.

Jetty on Esperance Bay. Photo – Bill Belson/Lochman Transparencies

WHERE IS IT? 721 km from Perth, 207 km from Norseman, 476 km from Albany, 402 km from Kalgoorlie, 187 km from Ravensthorpe. Daily air services are available from Perth.

TRAVELLING TIME: At least 7 hours drive from Perth or a 1½ hour flight.

WHAT TO DO: Fishing, walking, cycling, birdwatching, four-wheel-driving, whale watching, cruising, swimming, diving, beachcombing, scenic driving.

Great Ocean Drive: This 38 km scenic loop drive offers spectacular coastal scenery and takes in wind farms, Twilight Cove, Observatory Point Lookout and the famous Pink Lake. Head west from Esperance via Twilight Beach Road, Eleven Mile Beach and Pink Lake Road.

FACING PAGE
Top left: View over Blue Haven Beach. Photo – Dennis Sarson/Lochman Transparencies
Below left: Pink Lake. Photo – Jiri Lochman

WALKS:

Esperance Foreshore: A 15 km return walk leads along the Esperance townsite foreshore from Blue Haven Bay to the end of Castletown Quays.

Historic Walk: A brochure mapping the route and listing Esperance's historic buildings can be obtained from the tourist bureau.

FACILITIES: Full accommodation, shopping, dining and entertainment facilities. Scenic flights, sightseeing tours, dive and fishing charters and four-wheel-drive safaris are available.

NEAREST CALM OFFICE: CALM's Esperance District Office is at 92 Dempster Street, Esperance, phone (08) 9071 3733.

FURTHER INFORMATION: Esperance Tourist Bureau on (08) 9071 2330.

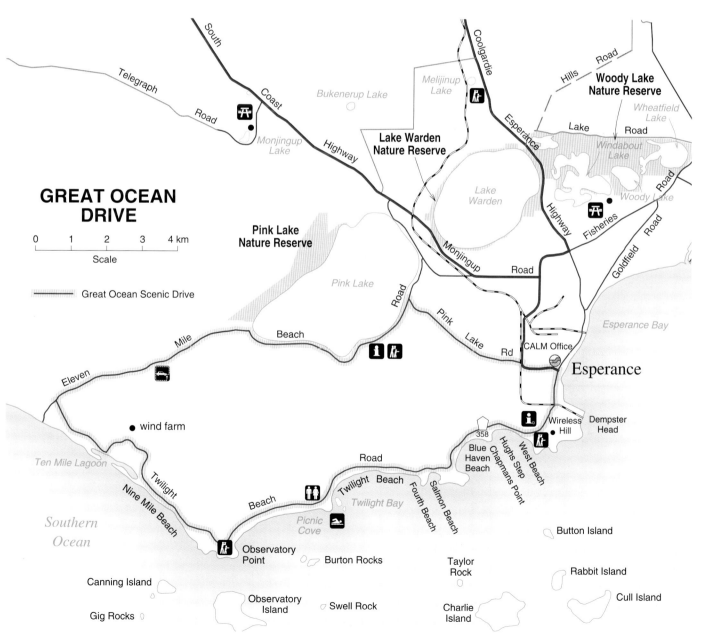

Esperance Lakes nature reserves

Five nature reserves, collectively known as the Esperance Lakes nature reserves, are located near the town of Esperance. They are Lake Warden, Woody Lake, Mullet Lake, Shark Lake and Pink Lake. Attractions in the reserves include the wetlands and coastal scenery. The wetlands provide great opportunities for sightseeing, bushwalking, picnicking and birdwatching.

The Esperance Lakes nature reserves are host to thousands of waterbirds, including two declared rare species – the Recherche Cape Barren goose, which is a rare subspecies with only 650 individual birds, and the freckled duck. At least 59 species of waterbird have been recorded in the Lake Warden, Woody Lake and Mullet Lake nature reserves.

In terms of numbers of birds, the wetlands are some of the most important in southern WA for banded stilts, Australian shelducks, black swans, chestnut teals, musk ducks and Australasian shovellers. Lake Warden, Woody Lake and Mullet Lake support more than 10 per cent of the total population of the hooded plover, an uncommon species restricted to southern Australia. The entire Australian population of hooded plovers is estimated to be about 5 000 birds.

Because of the conservation values of the reserves as waterbird habitat, and as an example of saline coastal lakes on the South Coast of WA, Lake Warden, Woody Lake and Mullet Lake nature reserves are listed as wetlands of international importance under the Ramsar Convention and are listed on the National Estate Register. They are also home to at least 17 species of migratory waterbird protected under international conventions.

WHERE ARE THEY? They surround the Esperance townsite.

TRAVELLING TIME: 10 minutes.

TOTAL AREA: 3 384 ha.

WHAT TO DO: Bushwalking, picnicking and birdwatching.

FACILITIES: Picnic tables at Lake Wheatfield and Lake Windabout. A walktrail, canoe trail, bird hides and a lookout are found around Woody Lake and Lake Wheatfield.

NEAREST CALM OFFICE: CALM's Esperance District Office is at 92 Dempster Street, Esperance, phone (08) 9071 3733.

Lake Warden. Photo – Steve Sadler

Woody Island Nature Reserve

Woody Island Nature Reserve is one of more than 100 islands in the magnificent Archipelago of the Recherche, which stretches for more than 200 kilometres along the State's southern coast. The archipelago is steeped in history, with pirates, sealers, whalers and sheep farmers the main users in its early days.

Woody Island is 130 metres above sea level at the highest point, and is the only readily accessible island close to Esperance in the archipelago. A camping area has been developed for people to experience the wonders of the island, which is a nature lover's delight.

The island is serviced by the catamaran *MV Seabreeze*, which stops there for morning tea and a short guided walk on its daily 3½ hour Bay of Isles Wildlife Cruise. During the cruise, you can see the white-breasted sea-eagle and view Australian sea lions and New Zealand fur seals in their natural habitat. Additional ferry services are available during summer.

Dolphins and seals visit the island, and wildlife residing on the island includes kangaroos, birds such as sea eagles, honeyeaters, finches and shearwaters, with geckoes and lizards galore. Shady eucalypts, melaleucas and sheoaks, sheltered sparkling bays and abundant wildlife add to the natural beauty of this island hideaway.

RECREATION

Visitors can either take a half day or day trip from Esperance or stay overnight. Accommodation on the island is provided in permanent safari-style tents, which include a double bed and bunks. These tents are on a raised wooden platform with a balcony overlooking the bush, from which you can glimpse Shearwater Bay. Standard tents are also available and all have foam mattresses.

A fully equipped community kitchen is available, and there is a well-stocked kiosk. A modern ablution block provides hot water for showering and laundering. Masks and snorkels can be hired for underwater viewing of fish, coral and wrecks. A glass bottomed boat operates for those who aren't keen to get wet.

Other activities include bushwalking, diving, fishing from two jetties, swimming, or just relaxing and soaking up the peace and serenity of this unique island location.

WHERE IS IT? 15 km from Esperance in the centre of the beautiful Bay of Isles.

TRAVELLING TIME: The half day cruise on the ferry takes 3½ hours.

TOTAL AREA: 195 ha, with about 30 ha developed for tourism.

WHAT TO DO: Camping, fishing, snorkelling, scuba diving, walking, birdwatching, swimming.

FACILITIES: Jetty, kiosk, interpretation centre, accommodation, toilets, mask and snorkel hire, glass bottomed boat, swimming platform and water slide.

FURTHER ENQUIRIES: Bookings can be made through MacKenzie's Island Cruises, 71 The Esplanade, Esperance, phone (08) 9071 5757 (all hours). Groups, including school groups, are specially catered for with flexible ferry times.

Woody Island campsite. Photo – MacKenzie's Island Cruises

Cape Le Grand National Park

Wild coastal scenery, rugged granite peaks and sweeping heathlands characterise Cape Le Grand National Park. The park has attractive bays with wide sandy beaches set between rocky headlands.

In the park's south-west, massive outcrops of granite and gneiss form an impressive chain of peaks including Mount Le Grand (345 metres), Frenchman Peak (262 metres) and Mississippi Hill (180 metres). They are the result of erosion and movements in the Earth's crust over the past 600 million years. Caves and tunnels found in the peaks are thought to be the result of waves and underwater currents during a period some 40 million years ago.

The park is named after Le Grand, an officer on a French expedition commanded by Admiral D'Entrecasteaux in 1792. Matthew Flinders named Lucky Bay in 1802 when taking shelter from a summer storm. Rossiter Bay was named by John Eyre in 1841 when after crossing the Nullarbor he found the ship *Mississippi*, captained by Rossiter. Mississippi Hill at Lucky Bay was named after the ship.

A party led by explorer and prominent colonist John Forrest also passed through the area in 1870. Frenchman Peak was named by his brother, Alexander Forrest, because its shape was said to resemble a man wearing a Frenchman's cap. The Aboriginal name for the peak was Mandoorbureup.

WILDFLOWERS AND WILDLIFE

The sandplains of the park support a great variety of wildlife. In areas of deep sand, dense thickets of showy banksia (*Banksia speciosa*) thrive, growing to three or four metres tall. On gravel outcrops, and in areas where the soil is shallow, scrub banksia (*Banksia pulchella*) may be found.

Many species of small native mammal rely on plant communities for food and shelter. Banksias are a source of nectar and insects for the honey possum, while the quenda forages in the understorey for grubs and worms.

RECREATION

There are two camping areas at Cape Le Grand National Park, one at Lucky Bay and the other at Le Grand Beach. Facilities include septic toilets and showers. A camping fee is charged.

Boats are best launched at Lucky Bay, but small boats can also be launched from Cape Le Grand Beach. Launching at Rossiter Bay is not recommended. These beaches are notoriously treacherous for vehicles. Ask the ranger about surface conditions or tides.

FACING PAGE
Lucky Bay campground. Below: Hikers in Lucky Bay. Photos – Jiri Lochman

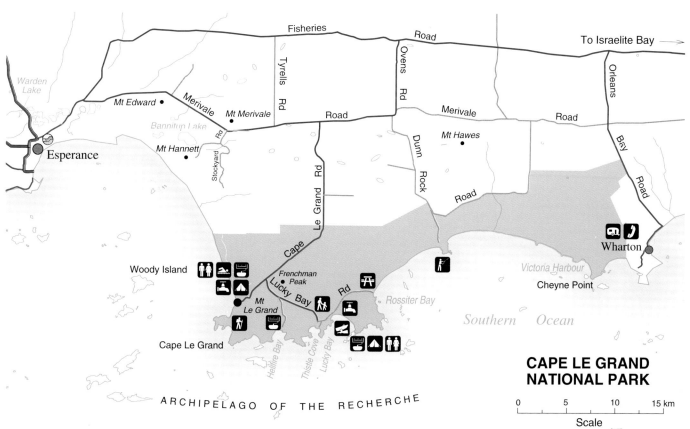

Fisheries Road To Israelite Bay →

Warden Lake

Mt Edward Merivale Rd
Mt Merivale

Bannitup Lake

Tyrells Rd

Ovens Rd

Orleans

Esperance

Mt Hannett

Stockyard Rd

Road

Merivale Road

Mt Hawes

Dunn Rock Road

Bay Road

Wharton

Woody Island

Le Grand Rd

Cape

Frenchman Peak

Lucky Bay Rd

Mt Le Grand

Victoria Harbour
Cheyne Point

Southern Ocean

Rossiter Bay

Cape Le Grand

Hellfire Bay

Thistle Cove

Lucky Bay

ARCHIPELAGO OF THE RECHERCHE

CAPE LE GRAND NATIONAL PARK

0   5   10   15 km

Scale

Cape Arid National Park

Cape Arid National Park is renowned for its sweeping beaches, clear blue seas and rocky headlands. Low granite hills extend inland, and in the northern part of the park the Russell Range rises to its highest peak of Mount Ragged (594 metres). Like the Barrens of the Fitzgerald River National Park, Mount Ragged and the Russell Range were islands when sea levels rose about 40 million years ago. Wave-cut platforms can be seen on their upper slopes.

Together with the Nuytsland Nature Reserve and Eucla National Park to the east, Cape Arid National Park forms a continuous nature conservation area almost to the South Australian border. The coastal heathlands have abundant wildflowers in spring. The park also has extensive areas of woodland in the northern sections.

In 1870, Mr Campbell-Taylor arrived to take up land around the Thomas River for grazing. Ponton and Sharp settled the area around Pine Hill five years later. The ruins of their buildings and dams, and the graves of some travellers, can still be seen near the waterhole at Pine Hill. In a deep valley east of Mount Arid, the grave of William Ponton and the remains of Hill Springs, the homestead of the Baesjou family can be found.

BIRDS AND OTHER LIFE

Birds include the scarlet robin, western spinebill and red-eared firetail, mulga parrot and pied butcherbird. Sixteen of the 18 species of honeyeater found in WA south of Dongara are known from the park, a good indication of the richness of species.

One critically endangered bird, the western ground parrot, lives in the park, and several rare species, including the Australasian bittern, Carnaby's black-cockatoo and Cape Barren goose, visit the park on occasions. Western Australian Cape Barren geese breed only in the Recherche Archipelago, and occasionally visit nearby parts of the mainland. Total numbers are estimated to be only about 650 birds.

In 1998, a number of endangered chuditch were reintroduced to Cape Arid National Park as part of the Department of Conservation and Land Management's *Western Shield* project (see page 12). Aerial fox baiting is carried out at Cape Arid and other parks around Esperance to keep down the numbers of these introduced predators and give native wildlife a chance of recovering.

Whales are regularly spotted off the coast, especially during late winter and spring, and seals sometimes visit the beaches. Western brush wallabies are relatively common. In 1930, a 'living fossil' was discovered in Cape Arid National Park. The world's most primitive species of ant, more primitive than known fossil ants, was found alive and thriving near Mount Ragged.

RECREATION

There are three main areas of attraction to visitors. In the Thomas River area, where the park headquarters are situated, there are excellent camping facilities, including several walks. This area is accessible by conventional vehicle and has good unsealed roads.

The Seal Creek-Poison Creek area is popular for camping and fishing, and is accessible by conventional vehicle via Baring Road.

The Mount Ragged area requires four-wheel-drive. It has a quiet camping area and a footpath to the summit of Tower Peak. Many species of orchid and several ferns grow on and near Mount Ragged, together with a small population of the sticky tailflower (*Anthocercis viscosa*), which is more typical of coastal locations.

Unfortunately, the plant-killing dieback disease (*Phytophthora cinnamomi*) has become established in some parts of the park, and vehicles must keep strictly to the signposted roads.

Ruins of Hills Spring homestead. Photo – Marie Lochman

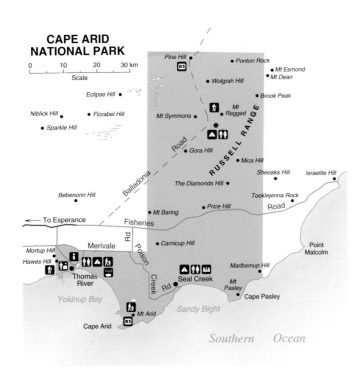

CAPE ARID NATIONAL PARK

0   10   20   30 km
Scale

Pine Hill
Ponton Rock
Mt Esmond
Mt Dean
Wolgrah Hill
Eclipse Hill
Brook Peak
Niblick Hill
Florabel Hill
Mt Symmons
Mt Ragged
Sparkle Hill
RUSSELL RANGE
Gora Hill
Mica Hill
Balladonia Road
Sheoaks Hill
Israelite Hill
The Diamonds Hill
Bebenorin Hill
Tooklejenna Rock
Mt Baring
Price Hill
Road
To Esperance
Fisheries
Merivale
Carnicup Hill
Point Malcolm
Mortup Hill
Poison Creek Rd
Hawes Hill
Rd
Thomas River
Marlbemup Hill
Seal Creek
Mt Pasley
Yokinup Bay
Mt Arid
Sandy Bight
Cape Pasley
Cape Arid
Southern Ocean

WHERE IS IT? 120 km east of Esperance. The best approach is by Fisheries Road and Tagon Road. A slightly shorter approach via Merivale Road involves more than 50 km of extra driving on gravel.

TRAVELLING TIME: 1½ hours from Esperance.

TOTAL AREA: 279 832 ha.

WHAT TO DO: Camping, fishing, bushwalking, picnicking, four-wheel-driving, whale watching, birdwatching.

WALKS:

Len Otte Nature Trail: Easy 1 km, 1 hour interpretive trail.

Tagon Trail: Medium 15 km, 4 hour return walk with magnificent coastal views. It leads from Thomas River to Tagon Harbour. Take care on slippery rocks.

Boolenup Trail: Easy 3 km, 1 hour interpretive trail to Lake Boolenup, especially popular with birdwatchers.

Mount Arid: Medium 2 km, 1 hour ascent to enjoy magnificent ocean views from the summit. A path is marked over the easy angled granite slopes.

Mount Ragged: Hard 3 km return, 2 hour walk ascends Tower Peak for a 360° view of undisturbed bushland.

FACILITIES: Barbecues, toilets, tables, campsites.

NEAREST CALM OFFICE: CALM's Esperance District Office is at 92 Dempster Street, Esperance, phone (08) 9071 3733. A ranger is stationed in the park.

View of the coast from Cape Arid National Park. Photo – Bill Belson/Lochman Transparencies

Nuytsland Nature Reserve

Nuytsland Nature Reserve contains one of Australia's great scenic features: the 190 kilometre long and 80 metre high Baxter Cliffs at the southern extremity of the Nullarbor Plain. These cliffs are believed to be the longest unbroken cliffs in the world. The reserve embraces a long coastal strip of land, representing both the high cliffs of the Great Australian Bight and the ocean beaches, sand dunes and sandplains at Eyre and Israelite Bay. Near Cocklebiddy, it extends inland across the Eyre Highway.

The nature reserve is named after Dutch explorer Peter Nuyts, who sailed this coast in 1627. The area was traversed by John Eyre during his journey from South Australia to Albany in 1841. It also includes some of the old overland telegraph line constructed in 1876.

EYRE BIRD OBSERVATORY

The Eyre Bird Observatory lies within the Nuytsland Nature Reserve and was established as Australia's first bird observatory by Birds Australia (formerly the RAOU) in 1977. The observatory is a lovely old stone building within walking distance of the beach, near the site where Eyre found water during his overland journey. It was built in 1897 to serve as the Eyre Telegraph Station. The telegraph station was deserted in 1930 and remained so until its restoration in 1977. The building now provides simple accommodation for visitors and staff.

Visitors are encouraged to participate in studies conducted at the observatory. Ornithological studies include bird banding, a weekly count of shorebirds and seabirds along 13 kilometres of beach, and a weekly census of birds along a two kilometre track in the mallee. Special studies have been made of the malleefowl, red-capped plover, southern scrub-robin, white-browed scrub-wren and the 15 species of honeyeater recorded in the area. Other biological studies include the nesting of western pygmy possums, banding of chocolate wattled bats in the Nullarbor Caves and winter whale watches. The observatory offers courses in the study of birds, mammals, reptiles, plants, photography, history and art.

ACCOMMODATION AND MEALS

Bookings to stay at the Eyre Bird Observatory need to be made as early as possible to ensure availability of accommodation and transport. The observatory has four bedrooms and two sleepouts providing beds, mattresses and pillows for 15 people. Three meals a day are included in the booking fee. Visitors need to bring their own sleeping bag, pillowcase, towels and torch. Day visits are possible for people in their own four-wheel-drive, but you should telephone first. As it takes three hours to do the return journey from the highway, an overnight stay is recommended.

WHERE IS IT? The turn-off is 16 km east of Cocklebiddy on the Eyre Highway, and it is a further 15 km to the lookout. Beyond the lookout, you will need a four-wheel-drive and at least 45 minutes to reach the observatory. This track follows the top of the scarp for 1 km, then descends via a rocky pass to the sandplain. The track turns south 1 km east of the bottom of the pass and the remaining 12 km to Eyre is soft sand and may require some deflation of tyres.

TOTAL AREA: 625 332 ha.

WHAT TO DO: Birdwatching, bushwalking, beachcombing.

FACILITIES: Eyre Bird Observatory, phone (08) 9039 3450.

NEAREST CALM OFFICE: CALM's Esperance District Office is at 92 Dempster Street, Esperance, phone (08) 9071 3733.

Baxter Cliffs at sunrise. Photo – Jiri Lochman

Eucla National Park

Eucla National Park lies near the border of WA and South Australia. The park's most significant features are Wilson Bluff, a high limestone cliff which provides a vantage point for viewing the spectacular sea cliffs of the Great Australian Bight, and the vast Delisser Sandhills. The local Aboriginal people are called the Yirkala Mirning, and 'Yirkala' is believed to be the derivation of the name Eucla.

SAND AND SALT WATER

Spurred on by glowing reports from explorer John Forrest of extensive grasslands at Eucla, three brothers from near Manjimup decided to establish a pastoral lease there in the 1870s. Instead of the good pastoral country they expected, John, Thomas and Andrew Muir had to battle hardship, isolation, constantly encroaching sand and lack of fresh water.

John and Thomas Muir were able to locate the wells which had been dug by explorers John Eyre and John Forrest. They cleaned these out, enlarged them and set up troughs for watering sheep. There was little feed in the vicinity, and sand had to be constantly cleaned from water troughs and even the wells. The brothers ventured west and east, noting the names of native rock holes. The information they gathered was of great assistance when the overland telegraph was built a few years later. John eventually perished there of pneumonia. In 1979, the Eucla National Park was created from land that once formed part of the pastoral lease they established.

The park is bounded on the north-western side by the Eyre Highway and a section of the old telegraph line which, when completed in the 1870s, linked WA to the outside world via Adelaide. The park has no facilities. Today, just outside the park boundary, the ruins of the Eucla Telegraph Station are gradually being buried in encroaching sand dunes.

Several interesting plants grow in the park's mallee scrub and heathland, particularly a species of daisy (*Senecio*) not known from any other locality. Two other species of plant, Batt's templetonia (*Templetonia batti*) and small-leaved native rosemary (*Olearia exiguifolia*), are known only from the limestone cliffs on the bight, while Forrest's pomaderrus (*Pomaderrus forrestiana*) is another uncommon species found here.

WHERE IS IT? 730 km east of Norseman, 1 300 km west of Adelaide.

TRAVELLING TIME: 10 minutes east of the Eucla townsite.

TOTAL AREA: 3 560 ha.

WHAT TO DO: Sightseeing, nature study.

FACILITIES: None in the park. There is accommodation, a roadhouse, police station and a nursing post at Eucla townsite, and accommodation and a roadhouse at Border Village.

NEAREST CALM OFFICE: CALM's Esperance District Office is at 92 Dempster Street, Esperance, phone (08) 9071 3733.

Old Telegraph Station. Photo – Marie Lochman

Index

FACING PAGE
Bibbulmun Track, Beraking campsite. Photo – Chris Garnett/CALM

CALM Offices

METROPOLITAN

WA Naturally **Information Centre**

47 Henry Street
FREMANTLE
Ph. (08) 9430 8600 Fax (08) 9430 8699
Open: 10 am to 5.30 pm every day except Tuesday

State Operations Headquarters

Technology Park, Western Precinct
Dick Perry Avenue
KENSINGTON 6151
Ph. (08) 9334 0333 Fax (08) 9334 0466

SWAN REGION

Regional Office

Technology Park, Western Precinct
Dick Perry Avenue
KENSINGTON 6151
Ph. (08) 9368 4399 Fax (08) 9368 4299

CALM Outdoors Information Centre

40 Jull Street
ARMADALE 6112

Ph. (08) 9399 9746 Fax (08) 9399 9748

District Office

Banksiadale Road
DWELLINGUP 6213
Ph. (08) 9538 1078 Fax (08) 9538 1203

CENTRAL FOREST REGION

Regional Office

North Boyanup Road
BUNBURY 6230
Ph. (08) 9725 4300 Fax (08) 9725 4351

District Offices
South Western Highway
KIRUP 6261
Ph. (08) 9731 6232 Fax (08) 9731 6366

SOUTHERN FOREST REGION

Regional Office

Brain Street
MANJIMUP 6258
Ph. (08) 9771 7948 Fax (08) 9777 1363

District Offices

Kennedy Street
PEMBERTON 6260
Ph. (08) 9776 1207 Fax (08) 9776 1410

South Western Highway
WALPOLE 6398
Ph. (08) 9840 1027 Fax (08) 9840 1251

WHEATBELT

Regional Office

7 Wald Street
PO Box 100
NARROGIN 6312
Ph. (08) 9881 1444 Fax (08) 9881 3297

District Offices

56 Clive Street
PO Box 811
KATANNING 6317
Ph. (08) 9821 1296 Fax (08) 9821 2633

1st Floor
13 Bates Street
PO Box 332
MERREDIN 6415
Ph. (08) 9041 2488 Fax (08) 9041 2454

GOLDFIELDS

Regional Office

Post Office Public Building
Hannan Street
PO Box 10173
KALGOORLIE 6430
Ph. (08) 9021 2677 Fax (08) 9021 7831

SOUTH COAST REGION

Regional Office

120 Albany Highway
ALBANY 6330
Ph. (08) 9842 4500 Fax (08) 9841 3329

District Office

92 Dempster Street
ESPERANCE 6450
Ph. (08) 9071 3733 Fax (08) 9071 3657

OTHER TOURIST INFORMATION

WA Tourist Centre
Forrest Chase (opposite the Train Station)
PERTH WA 6000
Ph. (08) 9483 1111
Open 7 days

Appendix 6

Glossary

Administering Authority
'The local authority or people carrying on a home'.
(1959 Regulations)

Children's Homes
'This can refer to a wide range of residential provision for children who are not in the care of their parents and there are a number of different classifications within the category of 'children's homes' '(Berridge, 1985)

'Homes provided by local authorities for children in their care, and homes helped by voluntary contributions'. (Review definition in Ch.2 The Regulatory Framework)

Remand Homes
'Institutions created to provide accommodation and care specifically for juvenile delinquents'. (Review definition in Ch.2 The Regulatory Framework)

Residential Establishments
'An establishment managed by a local authority, voluntary organisation or any other person, which provides residential accommodation for the purposes of this [1968] Act'. The Social Work (Scotland) Act,1937

Residential Schools
'Residential schools are ... defined as residential accommodation for children cared for away from home with educational facilities on the premises'. (A Kendrick, 'Historical Abuse in Residential Child Care' Appendix 2 of this review)

Secure Accommodation
'Accommodation in residential establishments that restricted children's liberty'.
(The Secure Accommodation (Scotland) Regulations, 1983)

Voluntary Homes
'Any home or other institution for the boarding, care, and maintenance of poor children or young persons, being a home or other institution supported wholly or partly by voluntary contributions'. (The Children and Young Persons (Scotland) Act, 1937

Institutional Child Abuse
'Any kind of child abuse described in the five categories as set out by the Scottish Office (1998), which occurs within an institutional setting:

■ **Physical Injury**
   Actual or attempted physical injury to a child, including the administration of toxic substances, where there is knowledge, or reasonable suspicion, that the injury was inflicted or knowingly not prevented.

■ **Sexual Abuse**
   Any child may be deemed to have been sexually abused when any person(s), by design or neglect, exploits the child, directly or indirectly, in any activity intended to lead to the sexual arousal or other forms of gratification of that person or any other person(s) including organised networks. This definition holds whether or not there has been genital contact and whether or not the child is said to have initiated, or consented to, the behaviour.

■ **Non-Organic Failure to Thrive**
   Children who significantly fail to reach normal growth and developmental milestones (i.e. physical growth, weight, motor, social and intellectual development) where physical and genetic reasons have been medically eliminated and a diagnosis of non-organic failure to thrive has been established.

■ **Emotional Abuse**
   Failure to provide for the child's basic emotional needs such as to have a severe effect on the behaviour and development of the child.

■ **Physical Neglect**
   This occurs when a child's essential needs are not met and this is likely to cause impairment to physical health and development. Such needs include food, clothing, cleanliness, shelter and warmth. A lack of appropriate care, including deprivation of access to health care, may result in persistent or severe exposure, through negligence, to circumstances which endanger the child.'

(Scottish Office 1998, Annex C)

CCI	Childcare Inspector
HMI	Her Majesty's Inspectors
HMIe	Her Majesty's Inspectorate of Education
HMSO	Her Majesty's Stationary Office – Official publishers of Parliamentary reports etc.
NAS	National Archives of Scotland
NHS	National Health Service
NSPCC	National Society for the Prevention of Cruelty to Children
SED	Scottish Education Department
SEED	Scottish Executive Education Department
SHHD	Scottish Home and Health Department
SWIA	Social Work Inspection Agency
SWSG	Social Work Services Group
SWSI	Social Work Services Inspectorate
UN	United Nations
UNCRC	United Nations Convention on the Rights of the Child